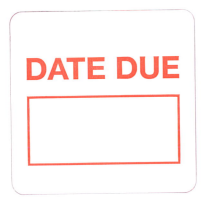

DATE DUE

The Black
Digital Elite

The Black Digital Elite

African American Leaders of the Information Revolution

John T. Barber

PRAEGER

Westport, Connecticut
London

Library of Congress Cataloging-in-Publication Data

Barber, John T.
  The black digital elite : African American leaders of the information
revolution / John T. Barber.
      p. cm.
  Includes bibliographical references and index.
  ISBN 0-275-98504-0 (alk. paper)
  1. African American leadership. 2. Elite (Social sciences)—United States.
3. African American scientists—Biography. 4. African Americans—
Biography. 5. Information technology—Social aspects—United States.
6. African Americans—Social conditions—1975– 7. African Americans—
Economic conditions. 8. Information society—United States. I. Title.
  E185.615.B297 2006
  305.5'23092396073—dc22
  [B]   2006018122

British Library Cataloguing in Publication Data is available.

Library of Congress Catalog Card Number: 2006018122
ISBN: 0-275-98504-0

First published in 2006

Praeger Publishers, 88 Post Road West, Westport, CT 06881
An imprint of Greenwood Publishing Group, Inc.
www.praeger.com

Printed in the United States of America

∞™

The paper used in this book complies with the
Permanent Paper Standard issued by the National
Information Standards Organization (Z39.48-1984).

10   9   8   7   6   5   4   3   2   1

Contents

Acknowledgments

I am dedicating this book to my loving and devoted mother, the late Nora Lee Barber. She made me into what I am today and what I will become in the future.

This book would not have been possible without the careful attention and editorial advice and assistance of my partner for life, Barbara Antoinette Gaston. I am also indebted to Spencer Hamilton, Sterling E. King, Jr., and William "Bill" Moore for their invaluable research assistance, administrative acumen, and editorial wisdom. Without them I would never have pulled it off.

Introduction

For more than four decades, African Americans have been leaders in the digital Information Revolution, which continues to change our world daily. This revolution has altered nearly every aspect of our lives by giving us cell phones, satellite television and radio, personal computing, the Internet, and the World Wide Web. African Americans have played diverse leading roles in bringing about this transformation from the industrial age to the information age, from building the foundation for Silicon Valley and designing the infrastructures for personal computers to crafting the laws and policies that guide this epoch of technological advancement.

THE ROLE OF THE BLACK DIGITAL ELITE IN THE INFORMATION REVOLUTION

Numerous volumes have been written about this era of advancement and the genius behind it. However, the technological contributions of Black Americans are seldom, if ever, mentioned. This book spotlights the Black digital elite, the African Americans whose achievements have contributed greatly to the advancement of the Information Revolution.

The Black digital elite are among the growing number of Black computer scientists, mathematicians, analysts, cybercommunity developers, activists, and businesspersons who are leaders in the Information Revolution. African American computer scientists and engineers, for example, helped to establish Silicon Valley companies that brought us new technologies and developed hardware and software, making it possible for this technology to reach all people.

Because of the impacts of the technology revolution on society, laws, policies, and new practices were enacted to govern the dynamic changes in American society. The Telecommunications Act of 1996 is the major legislation that supports the rollout of the information infrastructure of the nation. African Americans sat on the congressional committee that brought this important transformation of the digital landscape into existence and simultaneously headed up key federal agencies, such as Department of Commerce, Federal Communications Commission, and National Telecommunications and Information Agency, implementing new policies that made all Americans a part of the new age of information. Black politicians, policymakers, and political activists played a major role in this facet of the revolution.

Policies and programs established by the federal government changed the way that we educate young people and prepare them for occupations and professions during the Information Revolution. African Americans have spearheaded educational technology initiatives in California, Florida, Georgia, and other states throughout the nation. As the digitization of America rolled into high gear, states, cities, and communities throughout the nation worked to make sure that their citizens could benefit. Toward this end, African Americans led the effort to build cybercommunities in Atlanta, Miami, Boston, and other parts of the country.

Bringing the digital age to every household has been a major effort of the Information Revolution. Universal access is a key component to the success of the revolution if for no other reason than the facts that greater usage decreases the cost of technology and that when technology can become inexpensive, more people will buy it and use it. Much has already been written, for example, about disadvantaged African Americans gaining access to the Internet. Some of the Black digital elite are profiled here because of their work in bringing the Information Revolution to historically underserved communities and others for their lead role in drawing African Americans to the Internet with content that is for and about Black people.

In addition to getting everyone online, a critical issue over the past few decades has been how to use communication and information technology to enhance the nation's business and economic standing at home and abroad. During this time, African Americans have become movers and shakers in the corporate world on two levels. First, they shepherded into the digital era major mainstream companies such as AOL Time Warner, SBC, and Symantec. They also turned companies geared toward Black people into major corporate entities, such as BET Digital Networks and BET.com, Radio and TV One, MBC Network, and WorldSpace Corporation.

PROFILES OF ACHIEVEMENT

With the new millennium, the Black digital elite are making significant contributions to the advancement of humankind through the
development and use of contemporary technology. This is a story of
breakthroughs in computer science and the innovation of the personal computer, big business deals and the drama surrounding
media moguls and media mergers, and political wrangling to create
laws and regulations changing the landscape of communications forever. It is also a story of grassroots efforts to bring the empowerment
of technology to the average person in the community.

This book profiles 26 of the outstanding African American cybere-
lites behind these efforts, presenting their major contributions to com-
munication/information technology and communication/new media
technology and systems and their insights into the future of the Information Revolution as it relates to African Americans and people of all
races in America and abroad. Their profiles tell us about their contributions, life endeavors, and successes and failures. Their insights will
help us to understand what the technological future holds for us all,
the challenges and problems that the Black community in particular
will face, and solutions to these problems, among them closing gaps
in the digital divide, reaping a digital dividend for those who lack
access to the information infrastructure, and educating young people
to ensure their employment in a technological future.

Part I of this book, "Scientists and Innovators," introduces outstanding scientists who have made discoveries and innovations fundamental to the development of information technology. Part II,
"Policymakers and Power Brokers," focuses on African American
policymakers and those who influence information technology policy. Part III, "Educators and Professionals," profiles Blacks who are
educating new generations of people who use technology and who
are actively introducing African Americans to information technology careers. Part IV, "Cybercommunity Developers," presents a look
at Black leaders who are using cyberspace technologies to improve
communities in real space. Part V, "Masters of the World Wide
Web," focuses on the Black pioneers who have carved out a space
for African Americans on the frontier of the World Wide Web.
Finally, Part VI, "Chief Executive Officers, Entrepreneurs, and Big
Money Makers," profiles the leaders of mainstream corporations as
well as enterprises that are significant to the world of computer and
communications technology.

PART I
Scientists and Innovators

Computers are the driving force behind the Information Revolution. The term *digital* comes from the use of the numbers 0 and 1 to program computers to produce, store, and transmit information. The story of the Black digital elite begins with some of the computer scientists, engineers, and mathematicians who helped lay the groundwork for the information superhighway. The first elite is Roy L Clay, Sr., who was inducted into the Silicon Valley Hall of Fame for his pioneering efforts in the field of computers.

Presented next is Clarence (Skip) Ellis, the first African American to receive a PhD in computer science (1969). After receiving his PhD, Ellis worked on developing software for the first personal computers produced by Apple and then continued his work on supercomputers at Bell Telephone Laboratories. Dr. Skip Ellis has worked as a researcher and developer at Bell Telephone Laboratories, IBM, Xerox, Microelectronics and Computer Technology Corporation, Los Alamos Scientific Labs, and Argonne National Lab.

The third profile is of Dr. Mark Dean, an IBM fellow and Vice President of Systems in IBM Research. He was part of the team at IBM research facilities in Boca Raton, FL, that developed the first IBM PC. Dr. Dean developed much of the interior architecture allowing desktop computers to share information with printers and other devices. He holds three of the original nine patents for the PC's internal architecture. But that was more than 20 years ago. Dr. Dean's current work with computers promises to lead us to technology that will render the PC as useless as the eight-track tape player.

The last person profiled in Part I is best known for his many firsts. Dr. Philip Emeagwali designed the program and formula for one of the fastest computers in existence, the Connection Machine, as well as the system of parallel computers that is used by all search engines such as Yahoo and Google. Dr. Emeagwali also designed the HyperBall computer, which is able to forecast long-term global warming patterns.

Chapter 1

Roy L. Clay, Sr.

Chief Executive Officer, ROD-L Electronics

CONTRIBUTIONS TO THE INFORMATION REVOLUTION

In 2003, Roy L. Clay, Sr., was inducted into Silicon Valley's Engineering Hall of Fame for his outstanding professional achievements and significant contributions to the Silicon Valley community.[1] Located in and around Palo Alto, CA, Silicon Valley is the birthplace of the Information Revolution. It is now the home of 20 percent of the world's top 100 electronics and software companies.[2]

With his induction, Clay became a member of an exclusive group that includes Robert Noyce, inventor of the 8080 microchip and founder of Intel Corporation, and John L. Hennessy, president of Stanford University. He also joined the ranks of his former employers, Bill Hewlett and David Packard, founders of Hewlett-Packard Company (HP).[3]

The business relationship between Clay and Hewlett and Packard was full of ups and downs and ironic twists that led Clay to become one of the premier visionaries of the Information Revolution, and HP one of the leading companies in the information technology industry. It began in 1965 when Clay responded to a newspaper ad for a software development manager at HP.[4] At that time, Clay was attracted to the company because of its success and development of electronic testing equipment. After an interview lasting one and a half days, Clay was hired.

Hewlett and Packard had established their business in 1939, just after completing graduate school, with encouragement from the man often credited with starting Silicon Valley, Stanford University professor Frederick E. Terman.[5] The professor had envisioned the area around Stanford University becoming a center of excellence in academics, technology, and business. Having encouraged his students Hewlett and Packard to turn their idea for an audio oscillator into a company, Terman's vision started to become reality: HP became one of the first companies to fulfill his dream and one of the original "garage start-ups." In 1989, the garage where Hewlett and Packard worked on their audio oscillators was declared a California state historical landmark and is considered the birthplace of Silicon Valley.[6]

When Clay arrived at HP, the company had already achieved great financial success by creating and selling electronic instruments. Having worked as a computer programmer since 1956 at companies such as McDonnell Douglas and IBM, Clay felt that HP did not know much about the computer industry.[7] "At that time they really didn't know what they wanted to do in the computer field," he said. "They were mainly interested in using computers to manipulate data from their work with electronic instrumentation."

Clay soon became the guiding force behind the development of HP's Computer Division and forged its entry into the computer market. He was the first director of Research and Development and led the team that developed the 2116A computer and its software in 1966.[8]

In addition to leading the HP Research and Development Software and Hardware Group, Clay also served as its interim general manager. In this position, Clay did not just want to use computers for monitoring electronic instrumentation in the HP product line: he wanted to sell them. However, at that point in time, HP was not the computer giant that it is today. Bill Hewlett and David Packard had no desire to become involved in the computer market, leading to what Clay calls the "$22 billion misunderstanding."[9]

The disagreement started when Clay filled an order from Holiday Inn for a point of sales computer system. Clay managed and led the

HP team that designed this system, which included two parallel computers. Bill Hewlett instructed Clay to rescind the order and not to sell to Holiday Inn: "Terminate the project. We are not going to be in that business."

On August 21, 1971, David Packard told Clay to get HP out of the computer business: "You have done this company a disservice. You got us into this business and you have to get us out." As Packard explained to Clay, HP invested in products, not markets, and if they invested in computers, they would have to invest in markets. Clay responded that if HP did not want computers, then they did not want him. He subsequently resigned from HP. Clay and Packard did not speak to each other for 5 years. Looking back, however, Clay surmised that his most important contribution to the Information Revolution was "leading the team that created the HP computer system as we know it today."

In 1971 Kleiner Perkins Caufield & Byers, a venture capitalist group, employed Clay as a consultant on their investments in start-up computer firms that were springing up in the early days of Silicon Valley.[10] The firm decided to invest in the Holiday Inn project that Clay had been designing at HP. This business deal led to the creation of Tandem Computers. Tom Perkins, head of the firm, undertook another investment that later became Compaq. Compaq bought Tandem, and in 2001, more than 35 years after Clay recommended that HP pursue computers sales, HP bought Compaq for more than $22 billion.[11]

Although Hewlett and Packard tried to keep their company out of the computer business during Clay's tenure, today HP is renowned for its line of personal computers and printers and has also long been a leader in midrange computer systems.[12] With corporate headquarters in Palo Alto, CA, by 1999 HP was a $40 billion multinational organization. Over the past 40 years, the Computer Division started by Clay has helped HP become one of the leading success stories in American business.

After working for HP and Kleiner Perkins Caufield & Byers, Clay was unsure of what he wanted to do next. With the encouragement of his wife, Virginia, in 1977 Clay started his own business, ROD-L Electronics.[13] Clay is currently chief executive officer of ROD-L Electronics, the inventor of the automated dielectric withstand (Hipot) tester, and a world leader in development of electrical safety testing equipment.[14]

ROD-L Electronics is not directly involved with computers or other information technologies. However, the machines that Clay's company invented and sells are used by major electronic firms to test the safety of computers and electronic devices sold to American consumers.[15] AT&T Corporation, HP, IBM, Tektronix, Inc., and Xerox Corporation were development partners with ROD-L Electronics. These companies were the first users of ROD-L Hipot testers.

ROD-L set the industry standard in electrical product safety testing by producing the world's first Underwriters Laboratories (UL) safety-certified dielectric withstand (Hipot) and ground continuity testers and has since received the Consumer Product Safety Award. "Companies including Hewlett-Packard and General Electric use it to test their products—everything from computers to televisions to dishwashers to cardiac pacemakers—to make sure they're safe from electrical shock or fires," Clay explained.[16]

AFRICAN AMERICANS AND THE INFORMATION REVOLUTION

After leaving HP, Clay grew concerned over Silicon Valley's failure to hire more Africans Americans. He wanted to get them involved in everything.[17] With the start of ROD-L Electronics, however, Clay was able to make up for this hiring deficit. Having been honored by the governor of California as the founder of one of the state's oldest Black-owned technology companies, Clay continues to use his company to bring more African Americans and other minorities into the field of technology. ROD-L Electronics has been hiring Opportunities Industrialization Centers West (OICW) graduates since Clay founded the company.[18] OICW is a nonprofit community-based firm that provides job training for young people.

Based in Menlo Park, CA, Clay's company is a leader in youth development among African Americans and other minorities. ROD-L Electronics was the recipient of the "Dads Count Family Friendly Employer Award" issued by the County of San Mateo. In addition, Clay has worked for more than 35 years in Silicon Valley as a leader in community-based organizations with the objective of "improving the quality of life in the community."[19]

Clay predicts that in the future anyone who does not understand the concept of information technology will be at a great disadvantage.[20] He further deems that African Americans need to know what computers can do and that they are simple to operate. Since he mastered computer programming as early as 1956, he believes that

African Americans who lack computer savvy today simply need more exposure. "It's a natural part of our being," he said. "Just expose people to it. Just exposure to its components allows us all to do as well as anyone else."

When he left HP, Clay invited all the African Americans at the company to his house and impressed upon them that no African American would ever reach his level because he was one of the first Black managers. He cautioned them to keep in mind that "until all of us have made it, none of us have made it; therefore, we must support each other. You need a support group." Clay considers networking to be the most important factor for the success of African Americans in this country. "African Americans don't have networking and we need that," he said. "You have to be able to get where you want to go in two telephone calls."

Clay feels that the concept of the "digital divide" is a way of stalling African Americans' entry into information technology. Clay recalled that Bill Hewlett once said, "What African Americans need to do is what women have done. Learn to do something well." Clay recalled his thoughts when he heard that statement. "I said, 'Wait a minute. I was the one who started the HP computers. So how much longer do you need to wait?'"

BIOGRAPHY

Clay grew up in Kenlock, MO, just outside St. Louis. Kenlock was a poor town and the second Black city to be incorporated in the United States. He grew up during the era of segregation in America. Clay recalled that when he was young, he had to walk past the White church to go to the Black church. Kenlock nevertheless had a high percentage of Blacks who went to college, and Clay always knew college was in his future also. Many of his relatives had gone to college. They felt that education was their only salvation.

As a boy, Clay attended schools that instilled in him the belief that he could learn anything. He studied hard and was an excellent student. In 1946, the president of St. Louis University (SLU) offered him a scholarship. Because his family did not have money, a scholarship was the only way he could attend college. By 1947, Clay was a student at SLU with aspirations of becoming a professional baseball player.

Many college educators at that time felt that Blacks could not be educated. Despite his intellect, Clay was no exception to this mentality. He recalls that his chemistry professor once announced to the class that the person who got the highest score on the exam must have cheated. That person was Clay. Although he never cheated, that was the type of racial prejudice he and all Blacks faced in college. When he was a senior at SLU, Clay's family recommended that he teach or work in the post office like many college-educated Blacks did at that time. Clay had majored in math and wanted to enter the field of technology even then. He interviewed with McDonnell Aircraft, the forerunner to McDonnell Douglas. "Someone met me in the lobby," he recalled, "and told me, 'Mr. Clay, I'm very sorry, we don't hire professional Negroes.'" That was the end of the interview.

Undaunted, Clay taught school for a while in St. Louis and, on the recommendation of former Globetrotter Sam Wheeler, landed a job at McDonnell Douglas. In 1956, he became a computer programmer with the company and worked there for 2 years. At that time, no one knew how to operate the few computers they had. From there, he worked for Lawrence Radiation Laboratory, a developer of nuclear weapons, and later for IBM.

In 1962, Clay went to Palo Alto, CA, to create software and systems programming and established ROD-L Electronics in 1977. For more than 35 years, he has worked in the Palo Alto community to get more minorities involved in Silicon Valley technology and to improve quality of life there. He was the first non-White to hold the position of Palo Alto city councilman.[21] He said that he did this by networking with everyone. He served on the Palo Alto City Council from 1973 to 1979 and as vice-mayor from 1976 to 1977. An avid golfer, Clay joined the local country club at a time when it was still segregated.

Clay is tireless in his role as community servant. He has served and taken leadership roles in various local nonprofit organizations, including East Palo Alto's Girls' Club of the Mid Peninsula and the OICW in Menlo Park. He also served on the founding board of the East Palo Alto Junior Golf Program.[22]

Clay was married to Virginia Clay and has three sons: Roy, Jr., Rodney Lewis, and W. Chris, each an accomplished high-technology professional. Four years after his wife's death in 1995, Clay founded the Virginia Clay/Unity Care Annual Golf Classic to honor his wife's legacy of encouraging success among young minorities.[23] The golf tournament was established to raise funds for Unity Care's Pre-College Minority Engineering Program. Unity Care Group, Inc., is a nonprofit organization that helps Clay teach and encourage more African American and other minority youth to become involved in technology. Through the Pre-College Minority Engineering Program, young people are introduced to the latest technologies by designing and building their own technology-based projects. By staying actively involved in this and other programs, Roy Clay is helping to cultivate the next generation of African Americans who will be masters of technology.

NOTES

1. Silicon Valley Engineering Council. (n.d.). *Silicon Valley Engineering Hall of Fame for 2003*. Silicon Valley Engineering Council. Retrieved August 28, 2004, from http://www.svec.org/hof/2003.html.

2. "How it really works: What transformed a patch of prune orchards into the epicenter of global technology?" (1997, August 25). Retrieved January 31, 2005, from http://www.businessweek.com/1997/34/b35411.htm.

3. "2003 Silicon Valley Engineering Hall of Fame Inductee." (n.d.). Retrieved August 27, 2004, from http://www.rodl.com/rodl/hall_of_fame.html.

4. Roy Clay, Sr., personal communication, September 15, 2004.

5. "How it really works: What transformed a patch of prune orchards into the epicenter of global technology?" (1997, August 25). Retrieved January 31, 2005, from http://www.businessweek.com/1997/34/b35411.htm.

6. "Hewlett-Packard." Retrieved January 31, 2005, from http://searchcio.techtarget.com/sDefinition/0,,sid19_gci214558,00.html.

7. Roy Clay, Sr., personal communication, September 15, 2004.

8. Silicon Valley Engineering Council. (n.d.). *Silicon Valley Engineering Hall of Fame for 2003*. Silicon Valley Engineering Council. Retrieved August 28, 2004, from http://www.svec.org/hof/2003.html.

9. Roy Clay, Sr., personal communication, September 15, 2004.

10. Silicon Valley Engineering Council. (n.d.). *Silicon Valley Engineering Hall of Fame for 2003*. Silicon Valley Engineering Council. Retrieved August 28, 2004, from http://www.svec.org/hof/2003.html.

11. Roy Clay, Sr., personal communication, September 15, 2004.

12. "Hewlett-Packard." Retrieved January 31, 2005, from http://searchcio.techtarget.com/sDefinition/0,,sid19_gci214558,00.html.

13. Roy Clay, Sr., personal communication, September 15, 2004.

14. "2003 Silicon Valley Engineering Hall of Fame Inductee." (n.d.). Retrieved August 27, 2004, from http://www.rodl.com/rodl/hall_of_fame.html.

15. Smith, P. (2002, December 25). *Fully charged: Roy Clay, founder of ROD-L Electronics, keeps pushing for corporate responsibility.* Retrieved August 28, 2004, from http://www.almanacnews.com/morgue/2002/2002_12_25.clay.html.

16. "2003 Silicon Valley Engineering Hall of Fame Inductee." (n.d.). Retrieved August 27, 2004, from http://www.rodl.com/rodl/hall_of_fame.html.

17. Roy Clay, Sr., personal communication, September 15, 2004.

18. Softky, M. (2002, November 27). *Holiday fund: The OICW way still works.* Retrieved August 18, 2004, from http://www.almanacnews.com/morgue/2002/2002_11_27.ahfoicw.html.

19. Smith, P. Belle Haven: Improving quality of life.

20. Roy Clay, Sr., personal communication, September 15, 2004.

21. Silicon Valley Engineering Council. (n.d.). *Silicon Valley Engineering Hall of Fame for 2003.* Silicon Valley Engineering Council. Retrieved August 28, 2004, from http://www.svec.org/hof/2003.html.

22. Smith, P. (2002, December 25). *Fully charged: Roy Clay, founder of ROD-L Electronics, keeps pushing for corporate responsibility.* Retrieved August 28, 2004, from http://www.almanacnews.com/morgue/2002/2002_12_25.clay.html.

23. Unity Care Group. (n.d.). *Details of the 2004 Virginia Clay UGG Golf Classic.* Retrieved August 28, 2004, from http://www.unitycare.com/events/Golf%202004/details.shtml.

Chapter 2

Dr. Clarence A. Ellis

Professor of Computer Science and Director of the Collaboration Technology Research Group, University of Colorado at Boulder

CONTRIBUTIONS TO THE INFORMATION REVOLUTION

Clarence (Skip) Ellis received his PhD in computer science from the University of Illinois in 1969, the first African American to realize this achievement. This milestone, however, was only the beginning of a lifetime devoted to advancing the field of computing and creating ways to use computers to bring people together.

In 1970, Xerox Corporation founded the Palo Alto Research Center (PARC) in Silicon Valley and assigned it the mission of defining the "office of the future."[1] PARC sought to discover how office workers in the business environment performed their daily tasks so that Xerox could build better machines to help them do their work and to create tools that would help people work together.[2] Ellis became part of the PARC team of sociologists, psychologists, and computer scientists who built Alto, the world's first personal computer (PC), as well as interfaces, software, and languages,[3] which changed computing forever. The Alto featured the first what-you-see-is-what-you-get editor, a commercial mouse for input, a graphic–user interface, and bit-mapped display. It also included menus and icons, linked to a local area network, and stored files simultaneously. The Alto was the foundation for Xerox's STAR 8010 Information System. This advance changed the course of the computer industry and led to new ways of organizing interactions to support both individual and collaborative work.

PARC's original mission was also to create "the architecture of information." This resulted in quite a few groundbreaking innovations for Ellis during his tenure in addition to the Alto personal computer.[4] For example, Ethernet became a global standard for interconnecting computers on local area networks. Also, client–server architecture made the paradigm shift of moving the computer industry away from the hierarchical world of centralized mainframes toward more distributed access to information resources. Personal distributed computing was invented.

Ellis and the teams at PARC created these innovations in the late 1970s, but many of them (e.g., icons and the use of the mouse) did not become commercial realities until Apple Corporation turned them into business ventures. "IBM was not interested at the time," Ellis said. "They did not think personal computers would fly."[5] This occurred in about 1974; the first commercial machines did not come out until the 1980s.

Working on the development of the first PC is only one of Ellis's contributions to the advancement of computing. He has also performed groundbreaking work on computers that allowed collaboration among workers and an improved, more efficient workflow. Xerox Corporation founded PARC in 1970 to define the "office of the future." PARC sought to discover how office workers in the business environment performed their daily tasks so that Xerox could build better machines to help them do their work.

Ellis and Gary Nutt, his partner at PARC, developed Office Talk, a sophisticated and integrated system of office automation. Ellis and Nutt's office automation prototypes created one of the first approaches toward the automation of business processes.[6] They stated in their seminal paper on office automation that their goal was to reduce the complexity of the office workers' interaction with the information system, control the flow of information, and enhance the overall efficiency of the office.[7]

Ellis's work at PARC helped to usher in a new era in computing, and he continued to devise ways to use computers to allow people to work more effectively through collaboration. Since 1992 he has worked at the University of Colorado at Boulder to enhance under-standing of how computers can be used for collaboration.[8] There he has reunited with Gary Nutt and formed the Collaboration Technol-ogy Research Group (CTRG) to research topics of human collabora-tion and computer support for cooperative work. CTRG deals with theories, models, architectures, implementations, and studies and evaluations of computer-supported group activity.

In 1994, CTRG received funding from the Information Techno-logy and Organizations program within the U.S. National Science Foundation to research workflow systems, designed to assist groups in performing work procedures. Workflow systems "help an organization to specify, execute, monitor, and coordinate the flow of work items within a distributed office environment." "It's up to us people," Ellis said. "Do we use computers for destructive purposes like war and viruses? Or do we make the world closer together."

AFRICAN AMERICANS AND THE INFORMATION REVOLUTION

Ellis recognizes that although computers can be used to bring people together, unequal access to such technology serves to isolate them. Where African Americans are concerned, he feels more needs to be done to move Black people into the ranks of computer technology. "The 'digital divide' surfaced before the dot.com crash," he pointed out. "There was an effort to bring people into technology. After the crash, the digital divide became a code word for 'Don't hire Black people because they don't know computers.' When people were hired as digital divide people, they were first to be laid off because they were perceived to be less competent."[9]

Ellis believes that computers are migrating from personal machines to networks. The main use of computers, he maintains, is to collaborate, both with others worldwide and asynchronously in different time zones. Black people must gain mastery of computers in order to take advantage of global opportunities. The digital divide can and should be eliminated. "Let's find out what are the triggers that make students do innovative things with technology," he said. "We must become more than consumers. Blacks have to know enough about computers to say 'I want my computer to have a multi-cultural image. The interface should be Black and certain things should be done in my community. I'm not afraid of computers and I know how to do it.' That is where we need to get to."

Ellis is very optimistic about the future of African Americans and computers. He envisions two sides to the computing issue. Since he began at PARC, computers have changed from numbers crunchers to tools used by a much larger segment of the population. This segment, however, should include more African Americans.

The downside, according to Ellis, is that people are becoming more isolated. Young people are staying home playing computer games rather than developing social skills, even while this trend may cause Blacks to be good at consumption of computers and actively creative with this technology. To remedy this isolation problem, Ellis is seeking support from the National Science Foundation to establish initiatives that would make computing much more relevant to Black communities, so that they can learn more about this technology in a positive and social environment.

BIOGRAPHY

Ellis grew up in the rough neighborhoods of Chicago's south side.[10] Good family support and a lot of luck and hard work helped him to become what he is today. Marking his inadvertent foray into the world of computers, in the 1950s Ellis, still in high school, was hired by Dover, a large company in Chicago, as a night shift computer operator. As a new hire, the interviewer told Ellis that he was "the only one stupid enough to take the night shift job" and that "whatever you do don't touch the computer."[11] The company's computer, a huge vacuum tube machine filling several rooms, was displayed in picture windows for visitors to see. Ellis's job was to walk around and be visible so that no one would break in and try to vandalize the computer.

Dover had dozens of manuals for their computer, all of which Ellis read while working the midnight shift. On one occasion, a malfunction occurred that no one knew how to repair. Ellis surprised his superiors with his knowledge of, and ability to repair, the machine, gleaned from reading the manuals. Ellis was thereafter relied on for solutions to other computer problems.

At about this time, the University of Illinois started work on the Illinois asynchronous computer (ILLIAC). This computer had 3,750 vacuum tubes, and when turned on for the first time, caused the lights in the city to dim. Because of his experience at Dover, Ellis was called on to work on this computer and its problems.

As a student, Ellis had diverse interests, including math, sociology, and computers. In 1964, he received a BS degree, with a double major in math and physics, from Beloit College. As a graduate student, he studied computer science and received his PhD from the University of Illinois, where he worked on hardware, software, and applications of the ILLIAC 4 supercomputer. Computer science was still a brand new academic discipline, and Ellis was the first African American to receive a PhD in the field.

Ellis went to Bell Telephone Laboratories in New Jersey to work on supercomputing and then went to China to begin teaching computer courses.[12] He still teaches computer classes there in the native language, taught to him by his wife.

Ellis has worked for 12 companies and taught at 12 universities. His academic experience includes teaching positions at Stanford University, University of Texas, Massachusetts Institute of Technology (MIT), and Stevens Institute of Technology. He has also taught in Taiwan under an overseas teaching fellowship. At MIT Ellis worked on the ARPANET, a predecessor network to the Internet. He also worked on supercomputers in Los Alamos, NM, and has worked as a researcher and developer at Bell Telephone Laboratories, IBM, Xerox, Microelectronics and Computer Technology Corporation (MCC), Los Alamos National Laboratory, and Argonne National Laboratory.

In 1991, Ellis was chief architect of the FlowPath workflow product of Bull S. A. Previously, he headed the Groupware Research Group within the Software Technology Program at MCC. For the decade before joining MCC, he was a research scientist at Xerox PARC.

Ellis was invited to the University of Colorado at Boulder to work on computer-supported cooperative work (CSCW) in 1992. At the same time, he was asked to work at the University's Institute for Cognitive Science, where he started a journal and organized a conference. He heads up the research group as a full professor. The University of Colorado at Boulder is Ellis's home base, but he continues to teach in Africa and China.

Skip Ellis is one of the trailblazers in the field of personal computing. Still on the frontline of helping people to solve problems with computers, his current interests include the World Wide Web, groupware, coordination theory, object-oriented systems, CSCW, office systems, databases, distributed systems, software engineering, systems design and modeling, workflow systems, and human interfaces to computers.

NOTES

1. Palo Alto Research Center. (n.d.). *About PARC*. Retrieved February 9, 2005, from http://www.parc.com/about/default.html.

2. Hiltzik, M. (2000). Dealers of lightning: Xerox PARC and the dawn of the computer age. *Harper Business*.

3. Smith, D. K., & R. C. Alexander. (1999). *Fumbling the future: How Xerox invented, then ignored the first personal computer*. iUniverse.

4. Palo Alto Research Center. (n.d.). *About PARC*. Retrieved February 9, 2005, from http://www.parc.com/about/default.html.

5. Clarence A. Ellis, personal communication, November 11, 2004.

6. zur Muehlen, M. History of workflow research: From office automation to workflow management. Retrieved February 13, 2005, from http://www.workflow-research.de/Research/.

7. Ellis, C., & Gary Nutt. (1980). Computer science and office information systems. *ACM Computing Surveys, 12*, 27–60.

8. Ellis, C. (n.d.). *CTRG groupware and workflow research*. Retrieved February 21, 2005, from http://www.cs.colorado.edu/~skip/ctrgOview.html.

9. Clarence A. Ellis, personal communication, November 11, 2004.

10. Williams, S. (1997). *Computer scientists of the African diaspora*. Retrieved February 21, 2005, from http://www.math.buffalo.edu/mad/computer-science/ellis_clarencea.html.

11. Clarence A. Ellis, personal communication, November 11, 2004.

12. Clarence A. Ellis, personal communication, November 11, 2004.

Chapter 3

Dr. Mark Dean
Vice President of Systems Research and IBM Fellow

CREATING THE FIRST PERSONAL COMPUTERS AT IBM

In 1997, Dr. Mark Dean was inducted into the Inventor's Hall of Fame for his work on the IBM personal computer (PC), which set the standard for all PCs. Introduced in 1984, this device was called the personal computer with advanced technology (PC AT). Dean was also on the team that created the first PC at IBM, called the PC XT. He developed the color graphics adapter and the adapters that drove the screen, put characters up on the screen, and made the monitor work. His claim to fame, however, is the architecture designed for the PC AT, which was the successor to that first machine.

Dean led the team that crafted the PC AT, and his own efforts enable today's PCs to connect to disk drives, video devices, speakers, and scanners.[1] Dean and a colleague, Dennis Moeller, developed the interior architecture that allows desktop computers to share information with printers and other devices, and their improvements in computer architecture allowed IBM and IBM-compatible PCs to run high-performance software and work in tandem with those peripheral devices. This technology was first integrated into IBM PCs with the PC AT model and is now a key component for more than 40 million personal computers produced each year. It is often referred to as the industry standard architecture bus. Dean holds three of the original nine patents for this internal PC architecture. Dean's PC AT has impacted the entire information technology (IT) industry, but this was only one of many milestones in the career of one of the leading innovators in computer engineering in the world today.

"Most of the things that I have been recognized for, we didn't know (at the time) what we were doing per se," he said.[2] "We were working to make the PC a more general use architecture. We didn't know that we were changing the course of the IT industry. We knew we could satisfy some customer needs. We thought that we would sell a couple of hundred thousand systems. We didn't think that it was going to be a sustaining effort in itself. We didn't realize that we would list hundreds of millions of systems a year. We knew it was fun. That's the reason I was doing it. We were less concerned about changing the world than we were about building neat stuff."

MAKING COMPUTERS RUN FASTER

Dean has been creating "neat stuff" at IBM for more than 25 years and in doing so has been central to the design of a wide range of the company's computers.[3] Currently, he is an IBM fellow and vice president at the IBM Almaden Research Center in San Jose, CA. At this lab, he oversees more than 400 scientists and engineers dedicated to exploratory and applied research in various hardware, software, and services areas, including nanotechnology, materials science, storage systems, data management, web technologies, workplace practices, and user interfaces.

Before leading the Almaden lab in 2004, Dean was vice president for hardware and systems architecture in IBM's Systems and Technology Group in Tucson, AZ, and before that vice president for systems research at IBM's Watson Research Center in Yorktown Heights, NY. In this role, he was responsible for the research and application of systems technologies spanning circuits to operating environments. Key technologies from his research team include petaflop supercomputer systems structures, digital visualization, design automation tools, Linux optimizations for servers and embedded systems, algorithms for computational science, memory compression, S/390 and PowerPC processors, embedded systems research, formal verification methods, and high-speed low-power circuits.

In this capacity, Dean was the chief engineer on the development of a supercomputer called Blue Gene. This computer operates 100 times faster than the world's other fastest machines[4] and simulates how proteins fold themselves into their unique patterns. Solving this mystery of nature could have profound implications for understanding diseases and designing more effective drugs. With Blue Gene, IBM will set a new supercomputer speed limit: a petaflop, or 1,000 trillion floating point calculations per second. "One of my activities was to manage some of the initial work on the Blue Gene, which right now is the fastest supercomputer in the world," he said.[5] "And I don't see us giving up that title. We will dominate the supercomputing capability for the foreseeable future. We are now working on making it a more generally usable architecture so that it has more applications."

By partnering with the Department of Energy's National Nuclear Security Agency, Dean also led the effort to expand the design of the Blue Gene machine. Called Blue Gene/L, the second machine will be 15 times faster, consume 15 times less power per computation, and be 50 to 100 times smaller than the fastest supercomputers. Blue Gene/L is expected to operate at about 200 teraflops (200 trillion operations per second), which is faster than the total computing power of the top 500 supercomputers in the world today.[6] Dean believes that the design should be expanded to "deliver more commercially viable architectures for a broad customer set and still accomplish our original goal of protein science simulations."

Before "pushing the envelope" on high-speed supercomputers at IBM, Dean was one of the pioneers who made it possible for personal computers to operate at higher speeds. In 1997, Dean was named director of the Austin Research Laboratory and director of advanced technology development for the IBM Enterprise Server Group. In 1998, as director of IBM's Austin Research Lab, he led the team that built the first 1-GHz (1,000-MHz) chip, which did 1 billion calculations per second.[7] Achievements there also included testing of that first gigahertz CMOS microprocessor, design of high-speed DRAM, and development of the cellular server architecture, which is optimized for managing, storing, searching, distributing, and mining complex data (such as video, audio, and high-resolution images).

AFRICAN AMERICANS AND THE INFORMATION AGE

Not only is Dean one of IBM's leading visionaries of a great and prosperous new world for IBM and the computer industry, but he also envisions that technology will aid Blacks and others in becoming successful in the Information Age.

Dean believes two possible factors may help create a level playing field for African Americans. One is the way that people are trained to take on IT jobs and the other is a new computing device that gives everyone equal access to the latest IT.

Dean sees a time when young people will be trained in services science. He believes that services make up the largest part of business and will dominate regarding revenue in the IT industry. Services science would be an interdisciplinary field, combining human interaction, culture, and business, and would seek to combine the business, social, and technical fields, an entirely different approach than what has been used for the past 50 years since computer science was created. "Initially we hired math majors to program mainframes," Dean said.[8] "Now we need universities to graduate people in the field of technology services. We think it is time to define a curriculum that would allow universities to graduate people in services science. It's going to be a very interesting definition and curriculum. We are going to have to come up with a way to make that happen. We've got to get buy-in with colleges and other companies. It will change the industry and academia."

The Tablet computer is a technological device that Dean has imagined could replace the PC and help to close the "digital divide." This device will have the look and feel of paper, measure 8 1/2 × 11 in., and be as thick as Plexiglas. It would have the contrast, resolution, and flexibility of paper. In addition, it would be rugged enough to withstand abuse from a 5-year-old and would give the feel that paper is turning. "One of the reasons we have not gone to a paperless society is that all the displays are not mobile," he commented.[9] "They are heavy. We cannot stand reading a lot of material off computer screens. Let's design a computer that is a tablet and has the flexibility of paper." This Tablet computer would also play DVDs and CDs and would have all of the wireless services like XM radio. It could also do word processing and be a cell phone. Despite these impressive qualities, its most important feature, according to Dean, would be its low cost: inexpensive enough so that every student in every school could have one. The Tablet computer would contain all class work and homework and allow students access to the Internet. Schoolbooks would not be necessary; the Tablet computer would be the only tool students would be issued. "Now that would be one of the things that would level the playing field," Dean said. "If I give third-graders one of these, all of a sudden they have no constraints. They have as much access to as much information as anyone in the class. So we've gotten rid of one of the constraints, which is access to information. This would be an equalizer in minority communities."

Dean feels that this Tablet computer is not so abstract a concept and that it could be built in the very near future because most of the technology that would go into it is already available. Dean does not view the Tablet computer as a panacea and realizes that it will not fix the issues of inequality. "Technology may be an enabler, but we need people to be more 'color blind' because there are still constraints."

According to Dean, everyone must take responsibility for increasing African American involvement in the IT industry and for compressing the gap separating Black students, families, communities, and businesses from access to computers, the Internet, and the opportunities created by the Information Revolution. Dean believes that success in the Information Age is largely dependent on diversity in the workplace. He has outlined several key actions for success in closing the digital divide:

1. Educating young people in math, science, IT, and the opportunities available to individuals with this knowledge
2. Accepting information technology in homes, community centers, churches, and businesses
3. Implementation of a diverse IT workforce that mirrors the nation's cultural landscape

"We must act now," he said. "All the benefits of the information revolution await."

BIOGRAPHY

Inspired early in life, Dean never allowed societal constraints to hold him back from a life of achievement. He was born March 2, 1957, in Jefferson City, TN. His father was a supervisor at the Tennessee Valley Authority Dam and his grandfather a high-school principal. As a child, he and his father built a fully operable tractor from scratch. This type of positive accomplishment and the influence of his father and grandfather inspired him to great achievements early in life.

After high school, Dean received a Black Engineering scholarship from the University of Tennessee. He received a Bachelor of Science degree in electrical engineering from the University of Tennessee in 1979, a Master of Science degree in electrical engineering from Florida Atlantic University in 1982, and a PhD in electrical engineering from Stanford University in 1992. Dean said that working toward his PhD was as challenging as some of his technological breakthroughs.

Dean always wanted a PhD so he could teach at the university level and become an IBM fellow. In 1989, IBM sponsored his PhD. However, school was a struggle because it was an environment he had forgotten, having been out of school for so long. "The qualifying exam was the hardest," he recalled.[10] "I had 10 interviews with 10 professors on topics that they chose. They would tell you when you walked in the door what their particular question was. Only one of the professors in my qualifying group had a focus in computer technology. My particular interest was computer architecture. That was one of my most challenging and rewarding experiences."

During his career, Dean received an abundance of awards for his technological genius and community service. Dean was appointed as IBM fellow in 1995, IBM's highest technical honor.[11] He is also a member of the IBM Academy of Technology, serving on the Technology Council Board. He has received several academic and IBM awards, including 13 Invention Achievement Awards and 6 Corporate Awards. He has been published by the IEEE Computer Society Press and MIT Press and in *IBM Journal of Research and Development*.

In addition, Dean is a member of the American Academy of Arts and Science and National Academy of Engineering and is an IEEE fellow. He is the recipient of numerous national awards, among them Black Engineer of the Year Award from the publishers of *U.S. Black Engineer*, National Society of Black Engineers Distinguished Engineer award, U.S. Department of Commerce's Ronald H. Brown American Innovator Award, and was inducted into the National Inventor's Hall of Fame in Akron, OH. Dean has more than 40 patents or patents pending. With such a distinguished career, it is no wonder that Dean said "I've got right now the best job in IBM. It's a job I look forward to every day."

NOTES

1. Invent Now National Inventor's Hall of Fame. (n.d.). *Microcomputer system with bus control means for peripheral processing devices: Peripherals.* Retrieved February 26, 2005, from http://www.invent.org/hall_of_fame/38.html.

2. Mark Dean, personal communication, January 10, 2005.

3. IBM. (n.d.). *Almaden Research Center: About the lab director.* Retrieved February 26, 2005, from http://www.almaden.ibm.com/almaden/dean/.

4. Morton, O. (2001, July). *Gene machine.* Retrieved February 26, 2005, from http://wired.com/wired/archive/9.07/blue.html.

5. Mark Dean, personal communication, January 10, 2005.

6. Weiss, T. R. (2001). IBM to build second Blue Gene supercomputer. *Computerworld, 9.* Retrieved February 26, 2005, from http://www.computerworld.com/hardwaretopics/hardware/story/0,10801,65587,00.html.

7. IBM. (1998, February 4). *IBM demonstrates world's first 1000 MHz microprocessor.* Retrieved February 26, 2005, from http://domino.research.ibm.com/comm/pr.nsf/pages/news.19980204_1000mhz.html.

8. Mark Dean, personal communication, January 10, 2005.

9. Mark Dean, personal communication, January 10, 2005.

10. Mark Dean, personal communication, January 10, 2005.

11. IBM. (n.d.). *Almaden Research Center: About the lab director.* Retrieved February 26, 2005, from http://www.almaden.ibm.com/almaden/dean.

Chapter 4

Dr. Philip Emeagwali
Mathematician
and Computer
Engineer

GREAT MIND OF THE INFORMATION AGE

In August 2000, former U.S. President Bill Clinton stood before the Joint Assembly in the House of Representatives of Nigeria and proclaimed Philip Emeagwali "one of the great minds of the Information Age."[1] Clinton even compared Emeagwali with Bill Gates. In this now famous trip to Africa, Clinton visited Nigeria to help the nation move more rapidly into the Information Revolution. At the time, however, few knew of Philip Emeagwali, and many may have wondered what he had done to deserve such acclamations from a U.S. president. The Nigerian-born Emeagwali, who now resides in America, was receiving this praise because of the many contributions he has made to supercomputing and the computer revolution sweeping the world today.

Emeagwali won the 1989 Gordon Bell Prize for his significant achievements in the application of supercomputers to scientific and engineering problems.[2] The Gordon Bell Prizes are awarded each year to recognize outstanding achievement in high-performance computing. A purpose of the award is to track the progress over time of parallel computing in applications.[3] He won the coveted prize while a PhD candidate in the Civil Engineering Department and Scientific Computing Program at the University of Michigan at Ann Arbor.

His achievements have had a profound impact on the world of math, science, and engineering. First, he used a complex computer called the Connection Machine to solve an oil reservoir-modeling problem. He successfully implemented the first petroleum reservoir model on a massive parallel computer in 1989. He accurately computed how oil flows underground, and this made it possible for supercomputers to be used to find and recover oil and gas. At the time, this accomplishment was considered one of the 20 national grand challenges in science and engineering.

Another of Emeagwali's major achievements was a major break-through in the speed of computer calculations. His innovations made it possible to program thousands of inexpensive processors to out-perform supercomputers. He invented methods and procedures that enabled him to perform the world's fastest computation of 3.1 billion calculations per second in 1989 and solve the largest weather-forecasting equations with 128 million points in 1990.

He programmed a computer with 65,000 processors to outperform the fastest supercomputer, thereby proving that it is best to use many processors in designing supercomputers. As a result, the technologies of supercomputers now use hundreds or thousands of processors to achieve their computational speed. All search engines such as Yahoo or Search.com use Emeagwali's innovations in fast computing.

"The 65,536 processors were inside the Connection Machine," he said. "I accessed the Connection Machine over the Internet. The Connection Machines owned by the United States government laboratories were made available to me because they were considered impossible to program and there was no great demand for them at that time. In fact, the national laboratories that purchased them were embarrassed because their scientists could not program them and they were hardly being used. The labs were happy that I was brave enough to attempt to program it and the $5 million computer was left entirely to my use."[4]

A FATHER OF THE INTERNET

As early as 1974, Emeagwali was interested in using 64,000 computers, evenly distributed worldwide to forecast the weather. His scheme was called the HyperBall international network of computers. His peers initially rejected his design as impractical. He was denied funding and employment for a decade until the U.S. government's prime nuclear weapons research center, Los Alamos National Laboratory, approved his usage of its computers. Today, we call an international network of computers the Internet. When he successfully programmed 65,536 separate computer processors to perform 3.1 billion calculations per second, Emeagwali became world renowned. His work has enabled computer scientists to comprehend the capabilities of supercomputers and the practical applications of creating a system that allows multiple computers to communicate. CNN has written that this makes him one of the fathers of the Internet.[5] He has explained it in this way: "The Internet originated because the supercomputer created a need for it," he said. "The origin is the point where the computer gave birth to the Internet. That, in turn, was preceded by our understanding that many processors could be harnessed to form one supercomputer. Therefore, it was the supercomputer technology that gave birth to the Internet. The supercomputer is the father of the Internet."[6]

Future applications for Emeagwali's breakthroughs with the use of data generated by massively parallel computers include weather forecasting and the study of global warming. Emeagwali's use of 65,000 processors to perform 3.1 billion calculations, in part, inspired computer companies such as Apple and IBM to use his multiprocessing technology to manufacture laptop computers with peak speeds of 3.1 billion calculations per second.[7] Such companies now also build supercomputers that incorporate thousands of processors in their products.

AFRICAN AMERICANS AND THE INFORMATION AGE

Just as Emeagwali works to inspire great innovations from corporations in the computer world, he also works to motivate ordinary people to achieve great things through use of computers. He is particularly concerned about people of African descent being left out of the benefits of the Information Revolution: "An African American is three or four times less likely to be using a computer to retrieve information from the World Wide Web than a white American. In this Information Age where most information would only be available through the Internet, having a computer at home and work is as essential as having a telephone."[8]

Emeagwali recognizes that African Americans are overrepresented in those unskilled jobs that will eventually be replaced with workers with computer skills. Many African Americans are employed in clerical positions in the banking, accounting, and insurance industries, and these jobs will soon become obsolete. For these reasons, computer-based technologies will have a greater impact on the lives of African Americans than on any other ethnic group. Moreover, he feels that African Americans have less access to computers and Internet than white Americans. A group that does not have equal access to educational opportunities will lag behind the more privileged group. Similarly, lack of minority access to the Internet will create a "digital apartheid" that will keep them on the lower end of the socioeconomic ladder.

Emeagwali sees a multifaceted approach as the way for African Americans to solve the problem of the "digital divide." He recommends a change of governmental policies, entrepreneurial efforts, and investment capital. "We have to create computer and Internet training centers in the less affluent communities," he said. "We have to have all schools, libraries, homes, and offices wired to the Internet. African American families should invest in their future by replacing TVs with PCs. The Congressional Black Caucus should sponsor a bill to provide job training and financial assistance to displaced workers."

Emeagwali feels African Americans who desire high-skilled and higher paying jobs should make themselves more attractive to employers by taking computer courses at universities and using computers on a daily basis at work. Because computers and the Internet are the physical infrastructure of the Information Age, they should be as ubiquitous as electricity. "We now live in a global village and we have left the agricultural and industrial ages and are now entering the Information Age," he said. "We picked cotton during the agricultural age and rode in separate buses during the industrial age. We have to ensure that our children are not eating the crumbs from the dinner table of the Information Age. We must shift from only consuming technology to pioneering and producing it."

Emeagwali sees the future as a time that will be dominated by computers and technology. He predicts that 100 years, 200 years, or 300 years from today, "The Internet will remain a spherical network as large as the whole world. However, because it could be a zillion times more powerful, faster, and more intelligent, I believe that in 300 years the Internet will evolve into a SuperBrain as large as the whole world... Without realizing what we are doing, we are determined to redesign ourselves. Our compelling urge to redesign ourselves is deep-seated and will remain so. We have embarked on a self-propelled evolution in which we are both the creator and the created."[9]

Emeagwali believes that the Internet could be used to "unify the thoughts of all humanity. Unification implies that we will become one people. With one voice. One will. One soul. And one culture." He predicted that "our descendants will have achieved digital immortality in 10,000 years." Emeagwali considers himself to be "a Black scientist with a social responsibility to communicate science to the Black diaspora." In other words, he has a dual sensibility of being deeply rooted in science while using it as a tool to remind his people in the diaspora of where they have been and who they are.

BIOGRAPHY

Emeagwali's hope of a unified world of the future may grow out of a past in which he overcame war, genocide, and other insurmountable conflicts to become a great mathematician and computer scientist. He was born in 1954 in Nigeria. He was raised in the town of Onitsha in southeastern Nigeria.[10]

The capture of his hometown was the most prized trophy for the Nigerian army. Onitsha was the largest battle zone. In 1967, the civil war in his country forced him to drop out of school at age 12. Upon turning 14, Emeagwali was conscripted into the Biafran army. One million Nigerians—mostly women and children—died in the Biafran war. Emeagwali later escaped to Ndoni and volunteered to serve as a cook in the Officer's Mess of the Biafran Army. The Biafran army was defeated on January 15, 1970. Emeagwali was discharged and reunited with his parents. Later that month, he, his parents, and six siblings packed their meager belongings and, along with 5 million other returning refugees, started the journey back to Onitsha.

Emeagwali endured 30 months of living in refugee camps. He moved to Port Harcourt Road in the Fegge quarter of Onitsha. In 1970, he enrolled at Christ the King College, Onitsha. The school had been devastated by the war. "We used cement blocks from houses damaged by rockets," he said. "We used mortars and bombs as our chairs. I felt reenergized as a student."

Despite the hardships, Emeagwali mastered calculus and was known to out-calculate his instructors when he was a teenager. He often studied on his own because his parents could not afford to send him to school. His hard work paid off, and he received a general certificate of education from the University of London. At the age of 17, Emeagwali was awarded a full scholarship to Oregon State University where he majored in math. Upon graduation, he attended George Washington University and was awarded two engineering master's degrees, one in civil engineering and the other in marine engineering, and a master's in mathematics from the University of Maryland. He later achieved his doctorate from the University of Michigan in civil engineering. He also worked at the Army High Performance Computing Research Center at the University of Minnesota, where he conducted research on next-generation super-computers that will enable scientists and engineers to solve impor-tant problems in diverse fields such as meteorology, energy, the environment, and health.

In addition to the Gordon Bell Prize, Emeagwali has won more than 100 prizes, awards, and honors, including The Nigerian Achiever Award in 1994 and the Distinguished Scientist Award in 1991 from The National Society of Black Engineers in America for contributions to computer science and to the world community. Other accolades include The Nigeria Prize, Africa's largest scholarly prize, and Scientist of the Year and Pioneer of the Year from The National Society of Black Engineers.

Other awards include Computer Scientist of the Year Award from the National Technical Association (1993), Distinguished Scientist Award from World Bank (1998), and Best Scientist in Africa Award from Pan African Broadcasting. He has been profiled in the book *Making It in America* as one of "400 models of eminent Americans" and in *Who's Who in 20th Century America*.

NOTES

1. Clinton, William. "Remarks by the President in Address to Joint As-sembly." House of Representatives Chamber. National Assembly Building, Abuja, Nigeria. 26 August 2000.

2. Henderson, Susan K. *African-American Inventors III*. Mankato: Capstone Press, 1998.

3. *Gordon Bell Prize Winners*. 2000. SC2000 Conference Gordon Bell Awards. 12 March 2005. http://www.sc2000.org/bell/pastawrd.htm.

4. Bellis, Mary. "Interview with Philip Emeagwali." *Inventors*. About. COM. 12 March 2005. http://inventors.about.com/library/weekly/aa111097a.htm.

5. Christy, Oglesby. "African-American Feats in Science, Technology are Helping to Revolutionize Everyday Lives." *CNNfyi.com*. 9 February 2001. CNN. 12 March 2005. http://cnnstudentnews.cnn.com/fyi/interactive/specials/bhm/story/black.innovators.html#1.

6. Emeagwali, Philip. "History and Future of the Internet." Emeagwali. com. 3 June 2005. http://emeagwali.com/history/internet/.

7. Black Web Portal Newswire. "Dr. Philip Emeagwali: Father of the Internet." *Black Web Portal Newswire.* 6 February 2002. BWP.Com. 03 Jun. 2005. http://www.blackwebportal. com/wire/DA.cfm?ArticleID=558.

8. Emeagwali, Philip. "Digital Divide." May 1997. Interview with Toriano Boynton. 3 June 2005. http://emeagwali.com/interviews/digital-divide/computers-internet-information-technology.html.

9. Emeagwali, Philip. "Special Features: World Renowned Emeagwali— Metaphysics of the Grid." *Grid Today.* 21 July 2003. 12 March 2005. http://www.gridtoday.com/03/0721/101710.html.

10. Williams, Dr. Scott. "Philip Emeagwali." *Computer Scientists of the African Diaspora.* 6 September 2004. http://www.math.buffalo.edu/mad/computer-science/emeagwali_philip.html.

PART II
Policymakers and Power Brokers

The development of technological advances must be guided by policy and regulation if they are to be deployed effectively in society. In the 1990s, U.S. political leaders began to promulgate policies to regulate new telecommunications and information technologies that were impacting the nation on all fronts. The Clinton administration envisioned a national information infrastructure that would accomplish two goals: (1) promote the development of new technologies by creating a regulatory environment in which companies in the industries could compete; and (2) provide universal access to the Internet, World Wide Web, and all information systems brought about by the convergence of new information and communication technologies. African Americans played key roles in the development and application of legislation, policies, and programs that met the goals of information infrastructure realities in America and worldwide. Several of these digital elites are discussed in Part II.

The late Ronald H. Brown, former U.S. secretary of commerce, spearheaded the policy initiatives that led to the Telecommunications Act of 1996, the first major overhaul of telecommunications law in almost 62 years.

Larry Irving was assistant secretary of commerce and made the term *digital divide* part of the national language by conducting and publishing studies that showed that many Americans did not have access to the technologies of the information infrastructure.

Three Black U.S. congressmen sat on the House of Representatives Subcommittee on Telecommunications and the Internet. Congressman Bobby L. Rush helped to draft the original legislation that eventually became the Telecommunications Act. Congressman Edolphus Towns wrote the part of the legislation that created a Telecommunications Development Fund to assist African Americans in taking advantage of economic opportunities of the Information Age. Congressman Albert R. Wynn is leading the effort to reform the Telecommunications Act because its mandates have not kept pace with the rapidly changing information and communications industries in America.

Two chairmen of the Federal Communications Commission enforced the telecommunications laws that were laid down by Congress. William Kennard oversaw the information and communication industries at a time when there were more major corporate mergers than ever before in the history of the nation. Michael Powell initiated a period of deregulation to allow new technologies to continue to emerge.

Working outside of government, Reverend Jesse L. Jackson, Sr., challenged information technology industries to adopt policies that would result in more employment and entrepreneurial opportunities for African Americans in the burgeoning information technology arena.

Chapter 5

Ronald H. Brown

Former U.S. Secretary of Commerce

DRAFTING THE BLUEPRINT FOR THE INFORMATION INFRASTRUCTURE

During the administration of former U.S. President Bill Clinton, the chief executive and Vice President Al Gore shared the vision of a technological future in which all Americans would be connected to a nationwide, invisible, seamless, dynamic web of transmission mechanisms, information appliances, content, and people. This National Information Infrastructure (NII) would be more than the Internet. It would be a series of components, including the collection of public and private high-speed, interactive, narrow and broadband networks that existed then and would continue to emerge in the future.

When the president decided to put someone in charge of making this vision a reality, he chose his secretary of commerce, the late Ronald H. Brown, to do the job. Working with other government agencies and private sector representatives, Brown laid the groundwork for the emerging NII. Along with former Vice President

Al Gore, Brown put in place several principles that have guided policymaking for the Information Revolution that is still sweeping America and the rest of the world[1-3]: encourage private investment, promote and protect competition, provide open access to the network, avoid creating a society of information haves and have-nots, and encourage flexibility.

The Clinton White House formed the Information Infrastructure Task Force (IITF) to articulate and implement the administration's vision for the NII.[4] Brown was appointed chairman of the task force along with his regular duties as U.S. secretary of commerce. He delegated most of the staff responsibilities for the IITF to the National Telecommunications and Information Administration (NTIA). The task force consisted of high-level representatives of the federal agencies that play a major role in the development and application of information technologies. The participating agencies worked with the private sector to develop comprehensive telecommunications and information policies to best meet the needs of both the agencies and the country.

A high-level advisory council on the NII was also established by executive order to advise the IITF. It consisted of representatives of the many different stakeholders in the NII, including industry, labor, academia, public interest groups, and state and local governments. Brown led the team that was charged with articulating and implementing the administration's vision for the NII, the "information superhighway." Brown appointed the 25 members of the advisory committee.

Brown's work with the Clinton Administration, the task force, and the committee helped lay the groundwork for the most sweeping change in the communications industry in American history. Signed into law by President Clinton, the Telecommunications Act of 1996 represented the beginning of a new era in telecommunications regulation in the United States.[5-8]

This law reflected the new thinking of Brown and his working groups that service providers should be permitted to compete with each other in a robust marketplace that contains many diverse participants. In addition, the government must ensure that all citizens have access to advanced communications services at affordable prices through its universal service provisions, even as competitive markets for telecommunications services expand. The law also called for connecting all school classrooms, libraries, and hospitals to the information superhighway.

The NII would now become a reality as the communications and information industries moved to take advantage of the competitive provisions of the new law. The response in telecommunications and other communications and information markets began an era of technological convergence and merger mania. Four of the seven Bell regional holding companies, for example, announced proposed mergers: Bell Atlantic acquired NYNEX, and SBC acquired Pacific Telesis. The passage of time brought more mergers among the Bell companies and other local carriers as well as computer online services, media companies, and cable and satellite networks. While signing the law on February 8, 1996, at the Library of Congress in Washington, DC, President Clinton said:

This law is truly revolutionary legislation that will bring the future to our doorstep. This historic legislation in my way of thinking really embodies what we ought to be about as a country and what we ought to be about in this city. It clearly enables the age of possibility in America to expand to include more Americans.[9]

In the same year, Brown met an untimely death in a plane crash in the mountains of Croatia. At the time of his death, Brown was on a trade mission to expand American business opportunities abroad.

BUILDING A GLOBAL NETWORK OF NETWORKS

Before his death, Brown played a major role in the Clinton Administration's effort to spread the Information Revolution across the globe. Former Vice President Gore outlined the principles for a global information infrastructure (GII) in his famous speech at the first World Telecommunication Development Conference in March 1994: "Let us build a global community in which the people of neighboring countries view each other not as potential enemies, but as potential partners, as members of the same family in the vast, increasingly interconnected human family."[10] Held in Buenos Aires, Argentina, the conference signaled a new international initiative to establish an agenda to build the GII, using the following five principles as the foundation:

- Encourage private sector investment
- Promote competition
- Provide open access to the network for all information providers and users

- Create a flexible regulatory environment that can keep pace with rapid technological and market changes
- Ensure universal service

As secretary of commerce, Brown made the development of an advanced GII a top U.S. priority. NTIA's Office of International Affairs (OIA) took the lead in developing a GII action plan.[11] Under Brown's direction, OIA developed and launched the Clinton Administration's detailed action plan for developing the GII in the 21st century.

Gore's principles and Brown's action plan helped the international telecommunications community to formulate its own GII plans and principles. The United States has been successful in using this GII vision as a platform to engage foreign governments in discussions about the direction and content of their telecommunications and information policies and practices. By achieving global consensus on what telecommunications networks should look like and what the ground rules should be, the United States is better equipped to fight for specific changes in national and international telecommunications and information practices that will make it easier for U.S. companies to compete internationally.

ENSURING ACCESS FOR AFRICAN AMERICANS

Although Brown was known as a globetrotter who fought to create business opportunities for people around the world, he worked diligently to make sure that Americans got connected to the NII and the GII. Brown felt that African Americans could not afford to be part of the information have-nots in the future.

While Brown formulated policies for global commerce, he also addressed the question, "If information technology is a key to economic growth and global competitiveness, then what will happen to those that are information-poor?"[12] He felt that the way to ensure that all Americans could participate in the new age of information was to have the administration propose a renewal and reinvention of the concept of universal service. Speaking at the Museum of Television and Radio, Brown challenged a group of media executives to help connect all communities to the information superhighway. He was particularly concerned that African Americans have access to the NII in their schools: "I have increasingly recognized that their fate is tied to education and good schools." Brown challenged the businessmen to expand universal access to the NII: "That is not an obligation just of government to be imposed, as a distasteful act, upon business. It is an obligation of leadership in this society. Just as progressive businesses have increasingly recognized that their fate is tied to education and good schools, so the businesses that will take advantage of the new information marketplace must realize that our national fortune is dependent on our national competitiveness—on ensuring that no talent goes to waste."

Throughout the remainder of his public life, Brown continued to challenge leaders of industry to avoid creating a nation of information haves and have-nots.

BIOGRAPHY

Born in Washington, DC, and raised in New York City, Brown attended Middlebury College in Vermont. He served for four years in the U.S. Army and did tours in Germany and Korea. He earned a law degree from St. John's University, attending classes at night while working first as a welfare caseworker for the city of New York and then for the National Urban League. He spent twelve years with the National Urban League as deputy executive director, general counsel, and vice president of the Washington bureau. During this time, he became involved in politics and worked on Senator Edward M. Kennedy's presidential campaign in 1980. An appointment followed as chief counsel for the Senate Judiciary Committee under the chairmanship of Senator Kennedy.

In 1981, Brown joined Patton, Boggs & Blow, becoming the first African American partner at this prestigious firm in the nation's capital. He proved himself a skillful negotiator and was highly sought as a lobbyist. He continued to be active in politics, serving as the Reverend Jesse Jackson's convention manager in his 1988 bid for the presidency.

Brown used his skills as a negotiator and pragmatic bridge builder in his successful tenure as chairman of the Democratic National Committee from 1989 to 1992, reuniting the party after its defeat in the 1988 presidential election and leading it to victory in 1992.[13] Having earned a cabinet-level appointment in President Clinton's administration, he was named secretary of commerce.

He was the first African American appointed to the cabinet post of secretary of commerce and the first to serve as chairman of the Democratic National Committee. At the time of his death in 1996, he was a figure of global prominence, respected for his intelligence, political savvy, and leadership.

NOTES

1. Gore, A. (1993, December 21). Remarks from a speech presented at the National Press Club newsmaker luncheon, Washington, DC.

2. Farhi, P. (1993, December 22). Gore backs opening up data highway. *The Washington Post.* Retrieved January 21, 2006, from http://pqasb. pqarchiver.com/washingtonpost/search.html/?nav=left.

3. Electronic Frontier Foundation. (n.d.). *NII principles and actions: A checklist of the Clinton administration's progress: September 1993–1994.* Retrieved January 21, 2006, from http://www.eff.org/Infrastructure/ Govt_docs/nii_principles_progress.report.

4. Brown, R. H. *The national information infrastructure: Agenda for action: Table of contents.* Retrieved January 21, 2006, from http://www. ibiblio.org/nii/toc.html.

5. The White House, Office of the Vice President. (1994, January 11). *Background on the administration's telecommunications policy reform initiative.* Retrieved January 21, 2006, from http://www.ibiblio.org/pub/archives/ whitehouse-papers/1994/Jan/Background-on-Telecommunications-Policy-Reform-Initiative-1994-01-11.

6. Lamolinara, G. (1996, February 19). *Wired for the future president: Clinton signs Telecom Act at LC.* Retrieved January 21, 2006, from http:// www.loc.gov/loc/lcib/9603/telecom.html.

7. National Telecommunications and Information Administration. (1997). *National Telecommunications and Information Administration Annual Report 1996.* Retrieved January 21, 2006, from http://www.ntia.doc.gov/ ntiahome/annualrpt/96ANNRPT203.htm.

8. National Telecommunications and Information Administration. (1998). *The United States Telecommunications Act of 1996.* Retrieved January 3, 2006, from http://www.ntia.doc.gov/opadhome/overview.htm.

9. National Telecommunications and Information Administration. (1998). *The United States Telecommunications Act of 1996.* Retrieved January 21, 2006, from http://www.ntia.doc.gov/opadhome/overview.htm.

10. Gore, A. (1994, March 21). Remarks prepared for delivery in a speech presented at the International Telecommunications Union, Buenos Aires.

11. Brown, R. H, Irving, L., Prabhakar, A., & Katzen, S. (n.d.). *The global information infrastructure: Agenda for cooperation.* Retrieved January 3, 2006, from http://www.ntia.doc.gov/reports/giiagend.html.

12. Brown, R. H. (1994, January 6). Remarks from a speech presented at the Museum of Television and Radio, New York.

13. Holmes, S. A. (2000). *Ron Brown: An uncommon life.* New York: Wiley.

Chapter 6

Larry Irving
Former Assistant Secretary for Communication and Information, U.S. Department of Commerce

BUILDING THE INFORMATION HIGHWAYS

Speaking before the Television Academy in 1994, former Vice President Al Gore challenged members of the television industry to help build the world's information infrastructures.[1] He predicted the coming of a "digital revolution" that would connect the people of the world: "Today's technology has made possible a global community united by instantaneous information and analysis.... So it's worth remembering that while we talk about this digital revolution as if it's about to happen, in many places it's already underway."

In America, Gore's digital revolution was already happening because of the work of Larry Irving. In the Clinton–Gore administration, Irving was the assistant secretary for communications and information at the U.S. Department of Commerce and a leader in the efforts to bring about the Clinton administration's electronic commerce, national information infrastructure, and global information infrastructure initiatives.[2,3] Irving was also the head of the National

Telecommunications and Information Administration (NTIA), the executive branch agency responsible for domestic and international telecommunications and information policy. Under Irving's direction, NTIA developed and implemented policies that affected telecommunications and information sectors that made up almost 10 percent of the nation's domestic economy. At the time, these industries generated more than $590 billion in annual revenues.[4-6] At NTIA, Irving focused on two major priorities: promoting competition in the telecommunications industries in both domestic and global markets; and ensuring that traditionally underserved communities gain access to the national information infrastructure (NII) and the global information infrastructure (GII).

Under Irving, NTIA coordinated its efforts with those of other executive branch agencies through the Interagency Information Infrastructure Task Force (IITF), chaired at that time by former commerce secretary Ron Brown. The IITF included high-level representatives of the federal agencies that played a major role in the development and application of information and telecommunications technologies. NTIA served as the secretariat to the IITF, and Irving played a prominent role in the task force as chair of the Telecommunications Policy Committee (TPC), which formulated a unified administration position on key telecommunications issues. The TPC worked with congressional leaders to formulate effective telecommunications reform legislation that led to the Telecommunications Act of 1996, the most sweeping change in America's telecommunications law in six decades.

Under Irving's direction, NTIA also worked to ensure the deployment of a 21st-century telecommunications and information infrastructure that was accessible and affordable for all Americans. "Increasingly, getting a good job requires computer and technology literacy," he said. "Unless individuals have access to the NII, and, ultimately, the GII, either at home, at work, or through public institutions, they will be at a serious disadvantage in finding and keeping a good job." During Irving's tenure, the NTIA administered the Telecommunications Information Infrastructure Assistance Program (TIIAP) to lessen this problem by funding projects that helped make the information age accessible to all Americans. TIIAP provided matching grants to schools, libraries, hospitals, state and local governments, and other nonprofit entities.

The vast majority of the funds went to projects serving rural America and traditionally underserved Americans living in urban areas. The

Clinton–Gore administration strongly supported this program, but much of its funding was cut during the Bush administration.

On the international front, during Irving's administration, NTIA supported trade missions led by Secretary Brown that resulted in new opportunities for American telecommunications and information firms. One trade mission to China, for example, generated more than $5 billion worth of American business contracts, many in the area of telecommunications. Directed by Irving, NTIA also led the preparations for the U.S. participation at the G-7 Ministerial Conference on the Information Society in Brussels. That conference resulted in an agreement among seven of the world's economic leaders on principles necessary for the development of a global information infrastructure.

DISCOVERING THE DIGITAL DIVIDE

Digital divide is a popular term that refers to the gap between those who have access to information infrastructures and those who do not. Irving is widely credited with coining the term and being the leader who informed the American public about the growing problem it represents.[7–9] He initiated and was the principal author of the landmark federal surveys, *Falling Through the Net* and *Falling Through the Net: Defining the Digital Divide*.[10,11] Looking across racial, economic, and geographic lines, these studies tracked access to America's information infrastructures. The investigations found that Blacks and Hispanics had significantly less access than their White counterparts and that income played a major role in the level of access to computers and the Internet. Subsequent studies have shown that as the price of computers has decreased over the past decade, more Blacks and other minorities have gotten connected to information infrastructures.[12] Irving's seminal investigations were among the first and the most notable to bring the attention of public and private institutions to this issue.

TAKING IT TO THE STREET

Irving worked hard in this government career to ensure that African Americans and all Americans enjoy the benefits of the Information Revolution. He believes that government and private enterprise must work to ensure that African Americans gain access to the information infrastructures in this country and worldwide. In addition to gaining access, more African Americans must be hired in information technology industries.[13,14]

Leaders of prominent high-tech companies tell me they can't find people of color who are qualified engineers. But when I speak to human resources people, they tell me that practically eighty percent of the jobs in those companies don't require technical skills. That means something else is going on. It may not be overt racism, but there is no real outreach to the minority community, and high-tech companies need to work on this.

Irving also believes that the information technology industry can do more to attract African Americans to computer products. According to Irving, high-tech companies must do a better job of marketing their products directly to minorities. Computer ads are conspicuously absent in magazines targeted to African Americans, such as *Ebony, Essence,* and *Black Enterprise*: "The marketing departments of these companies assume Blacks don't buy computers, Hispanics don't buy computers. But if these guys had a clue, they'd start marketing laptops to people of color. Why don't these companies talk to hip-hop stars, fashion leaders, and create a laptop with a little style to it instead of making it all about wearing khakis and a poorly fitting T-shirt?"

Irving has entered into a joint venture with basketball legend Magic Johnson to form a business drawing people to the Net. As chief executive officer of the new venture, Irving continues to work to bring more African Americans to the new digital age.

BIOGRAPHY

Irving grew up in New York City and went to public school there. He went off to college at Northwestern when he was 17.[15] He received a Bachelor of Arts from Northwestern University in 1976 and a Juris Doctor from Stanford University School of Law, where he was the 1979 class president.[16,17]

For three years, Irving was associated with the Washington, DC, law firm of Hogan and Hartson, specializing in communications law, antitrust law, and commercial litigation. Irving served for ten years on Capitol Hill, most recently as senior counsel to the U.S. House of Representatives Subcommittee on Telecommunications and Finance. He also served as legislative director, counsel, and acting chief of staff to the late Congressman Mickey Leland (D-Texas).

Irving served for almost 7 years as assistant secretary of commerce for communications and information, where he was a principal advisor to the president, vice president, and secretary of commerce on domestic and international communications and information policy issues and supervised programs that award grants to extend the reach of advanced telecommunications technologies to underserved areas.

In recognition of his work to promote policies and develop programs to ensure equitable access to advanced telecommunication and information technologies, Irving was named one of the 50 most influential persons in the Year of the Internet by *Newsweek* magazine, which described him as the "conscience of the Internet." Irving was proclaimed a "technology champion" by the Congressional Black Caucus and received the James Madison Award from the American Library Association and the Mickey Leland Humanitarian Award from the National Association for Minorities in Communications. He also was recognized for his efforts to bridge the digital divide by, among others, the Alliance for Public Technology, National Association of Telecommunications Professionals, and Indigenous Broadcast Center of Anchorage, AK.

Irving is the president of the Irving Information Group, a consulting firm providing strategic planning and market development services to international telecommunications and information technology companies. He formed the company in October 1999. He currently serves as a cofounder of UrbanMagic and a member of the boards of directors of Covad Communications, Worldgate Communications, and Anticipa LLC. He also serves on the board of directors for TrustE; the advisory boards of Plugged In, Intel's Computer Clubhouse, and the Digital Blackboard Foundation; Advisory Council for the Law, Science, and Technology Program at Stanford Law School; and the Board of Visitors for the Weinberg College of Arts and Sciences of Northwestern University.

Irving is married to Leslie Annett Wiley and resides in Washington, DC.

NOTES

1. Gore, A. (1994, January 11). Remarks by Vice President Al Gore. Speech presented to the Television Academy, Los Angeles.

2. Gilliam, D. (1995, June 24). New gurus offer rides on info highway. *The Washington Post*. Retrieved January 21, 2006, from http://pqasb.pqarchiver.com/washingtonpost/search.html/?nav=left.

3. McLaughlin, G. J. (2005, April 11). *CRS report for Congress: The National Telecommunications and Information Administration: Budget, programs, and issues*. Retrieved January 21, 2006, from www.fas.org/sgp/crs/misc/RS21469.pdf.

4. Irving, L. (1995, March 22). Testimony of Larry Irving: Fiscal year 1996 NTIA appropriations: Subcommittee on Commerce, Justice, State, the Judiciary, and Related Agencies. Presented to the House of Representatives, Washington, DC.

5. Irving, L. (1999, February 18). Defining government's role in the new telecommunications landscape. Speech presented at the Third Annual Florida Communications Policy Symposium, Tallahassee.

6. Irving, L. (1995, March 2). Testimony of Larry Irving on telecommunications policy reform legislation: Committee on Commerce, Science and Transportation. Presented to the United States Senate, Washington, DC.

7. Irving, L. (1999, July 8). Remarks from a speech presented to the National Press Club. Washington, DC.

8. Cisler, S. (2000, January 16). Hot button: Online haves vs. have-nots. *San Jose Mercury News*. Retrieved January 21, 2006, from http://www.mercurynews.com/mld/mercurynews/.

9. Morino Institute. (n.d.). *From access to outcomes: Digital Divide Report: Larry Irving*. Retrieved January 21, 2006, from http://www.morino.org/divides/bio_irving.htm.

10. Brown, R. H. (1995, July). *Falling through the Net: A survey of the "have nots" in rural and urban America*. Retrieved January 21, 2006, from http://www.ntia.doc.gov/ntiahome/fallingthru.html.

11. Irving, L. (n.d.). *Falling through the Net: Defining the digital divide*. National Telecommunications and Information Administration. Retrieved January 23, 2006, from http://www.ntia.doc.gov/ntiahome/fttn99.

12. National Telecommunications and Information Administration (2004, September). *A nation online: Entering the broadband age*. Retrieved January 23, 2006, from http://www.ntia.doc.gov/reports/anol/.

13. Nowak, N. (n.d.). *Taking it to the streets*. Retrieved January 21, 2006, from http://www.law.stanford.edu/publications/lawyer/issues/57/feature2.html.

14. McGuire, D. (2000, April 5). Ex-commerce official impressed by digital divide response. *The Washington Post*. Retrieved January 21, 2006, from http://www.washingtonpost.com/wp-dyn/content/technology/index.html.

15. Educom Review Staff. (1997, March). Raising the bar on universal service: Larry Irving interview. *Educom Review*. Retrieved January 21, 2006, from http://64.233.187.104/search?q=cache:dcDcRRKquOEJ:www.educause.edu/pub/er/review/reviewArticles/32234.html+:Larry+Irving%22&hl=en.

16. National Telecommunications and Information Administration, (n.d.). *Biographical sketch of Larry Irving*. Retrieved January 21, 2006, from http://www.ntia.doc.gov/ntiahome/archive/irvbio.html.

17. Miller, B. (1996, February 1). Larry Irving. *Government Technology*. Retrieved January 21, 2006, from http://www.govtech.net/magazine/story.php?id=95559&issue=2:1996.

Chapter 7

Bobby L. Rush

U.S. Representative,
First Congressional
District, Illinois

WRITING LEGISLATION FOR THE INFORMATION AGE

Speaking before the Computer & Communications Industry Association on June 10, 1996, U.S. Congressman John D. Dingell said that he had some good news and bad[1]: "The bad news is that the 104th Congress has accomplished precious little of significance. The good news is that perhaps the only exception to that statement is our passage of the most important piece of telecommunications legislation in six decades." As the ranking member of the U.S. House of Representatives Subcommittee on Telecommunications and the Internet, Dingell was speaking about the Telecommunications Act of 1996.

U.S. Congressman Bobby L. Rush played a key role in the development of telecommunications legislative reform, which led to the 1996 law of which Dingell spoke.[2] Rush also sits on the Subcommittee on Telecommunications and the Internet, which is responsible for interstate and foreign telecommunications, including information transmission by broadcast, radio, wire, microwave, satellite, or other mode. This committee oversees homeland security-related aspects of the foregoing, including cybersecurity. He was appointed to the House–Senate Conference Committee on the Communications Act of 1995 and was engaged in the largest rewrite in history of the nation's telecommunications laws. He authored provisions in the Communications Act of 1995 that sought to eliminate market entry barriers for entrepreneurs and small business owners who want to be active players in the telecommunications industry. He also authored and sponsored legislation that would include African Americans and other minorities in the economic benefits of the Information Revolution.[3,4]

WIRING THE SCHOOLS FOR THE INTERNET

The Telecommunications Act of 1996 established a program entitled the Education Rate program, or E-Rate as it is popularly called. Designed as part of the universal service provisions of the Telecommunications Act, the E-Rate provides discounts of 20 to 90 percent on telecommunications, internal connections, and advanced services, including Internet access, to schools and libraries. From his powerful position as a member of the House communications subcommittee, Rush works to ensure that American schoolchildren will also reap the benefits of the Information Revolution. He has been one of the more active defenders of the Federal Communications Commission's (FCC) handling of the E-Rate program for subsidizing computer networking, telephone services, and Internet access for schools and libraries.[5,6]

The E-Rate was funded by the telecommunications industry, but some telecommunication companies wanted the program terminated. Under the telecommunications act, the industry is to recoup its contributions through lower local access charges and expanded market share as schools and libraries expand their telecommunications infrastructure under the program. Rush's advocacy for the program helped to keep it alive when it was under fire from critics. "This E-Rate program is absolutely essential," Rush said. "You know if you go into any urban area anywhere in this nation and you walk into an urban school for the most part you will see students there who have no idea about the kind of information available to them, have no idea about how they are being educated, about how they are being shortchanged, by not having access to computers, by not having access to the latest technology, and that that there is no other battle that is nobler than this particular battle as we move forward to make sure and protect the E-Rate." In its first 3 years, the FCC-administered E-Rate distributed more than $5.85 billion in discounts to telecommunications providers and other eligible entities for services to schools and libraries.

PROVIDING OPPORTUNITY FOR AFRICAN AMERICANS

Rush believes that access to computers and the Internet is fundamental to success in the future and that African Americans must gain the training necessary to be successful in the Information Age.

This battle we are engaging in right now is the civil rights battle of the 1990s and of the future. There are millions of youngsters who are struggling right now to become a part of American society, struggling to become productive in the American society, who are fighting without any of the technological advantages that are available to others. These individuals will soon be roadkill on the information superhighway because they won't have access to the kind of technology, access to computers, and access to the Internet. They won't be productive members of society. If in fact this E-Rate is diminished or ... if it's derailed then we are really creating two different societies.[7]

On Capitol Hill, Rush is a member of the Congressional Black Caucus (CBC), which recognizes technology as one of the most important issues minorities must address over the next decade. Rush takes the position of the CBC that African American workers must be trained to take the high-tech, high-wage jobs of the new information economy.[8] He believes that high-tech training grants should be provided to African Americans, who are now underrepresented in the high-tech industry. In his hometown of Chicago, the Bobby L. Rush Center for Community Technology has been established by the Rebirth of Englewood Community Development Corporation to provide computer training to residents of Chicago's South Side.[9] At the opening ceremony in 2003 Rush said:

This tech center would level the playing field for economically disadvantaged students and the unemployed so that they may one day enter the field of high technology. Many communities across this nation have been mostly absent from the high-tech revolution. This technology center will help to remedy this problem by giving community residents a chance to become competitive.

The center was established with a grant from the SBC Foundation. The technology center programs for residents include computer skills instruction, hardware installation and repair classes, employment placement, and a youth program designed to develop hardware and software proficiency. The center's economic development focus provides business technology training and serves as an incubation site for start-up businesses and a resource center for office and technology services for South Side businesses.

BIOGRAPHY

Congressman Rush was born on November 23, 1946, in Albany, GA.[10] His family later moved to Chicago and lived on the Near North and West Sides. Rush attended Marshall High School and at the age of 17 enlisted in the U.S. Army. He served in the military from 1963 until 1968, receiving an honorable discharge.

Following his military service, Rush attended Roosevelt University, where he received a bachelor's degree in general studies in 1973 with honors. In 1994, he received a master's degree in political science from the University of Illinois at Chicago. Congressman Rush received his second master's degree in 1998 in theological studies from McCormick Seminary and soon thereafter became an ordained Baptist minister.

During the civil rights movement of the 1960s, Congressman Rush worked to secure basic civil and human rights for African Americans, women, and other minorities. He was a member of the Student Non-Violent Coordinating Committee from 1966 to 1968. Congressman Rush was a cofounder of the Illinois Black Panther Party in 1968.

As a Black Panther, he operated the Panther Party's Free Breakfast for Children program. He also coordinated the Free Medical Clinic, which developed the nation's first mass sickle cell anemia testing program. This visionary Panther initiative forced America's health care providers to recognize the impact of sickle cell anemia on the Black community and to develop national research into its causes, effects, and solutions, a practice that endures to this day.

Before his election to Congress, Rush was an alderman on the Chicago City Council. He represented the second ward on Chicago's South Side for 8 years. As an alderman, Rush helped pass significant environmental protection, gun control, and neighborhood development legislation.

Congressman Rush received an honorary doctorate degree from the Virginia University of Lynchburg. He is the pastor of Beloved Community Christian Church and has been married to his wife, Carolyn, for 25 years.

Now in his seventh term in the U.S. Congress, Rush is a member of the powerful House Committee on Energy and Commerce. He serves on three subcommittees: the Subcommittee on Commerce, Trade, and Consumer Protection, Subcommittee on Telecommunications and the Internet, and the Subcommittee on Health. Congressman Rush is also a cochair of the Congressional Biotech Caucus.

Throughout his congressional career, Rush's leadership has been recognized and rewarded. As a freshman lawmaker, the Democratic leadership appointed Rush to serve as part of the whip organization, a position he still holds. His Democratic colleagues also elected him class president for two terms in the class of 1992.

Congressman Rush has taken the lead on a wide range of issues affecting the First Congressional District of Illinois and the nation. In the 108th Congress, Representative Rush authored the bill, H.R. 846, which provides for research on and services for individuals with postpartum depression and psychosis. The bill was named for Chicago native Melanie Blocker-Stokes. A significant milestone was made on September 29, 2004, when a congressional hearing was held to hear expert testimony as well as a personal account of postpartum depression by the mother of Blocker-Stokes.

On August 9, 2004, Congress passed Rush's bill to redesignate two facilities of the U.S. Postal Service in the First Congressional District as the James E. Worsham Post Office and the James E. Worsham Carrier Annex Building, respectively. On November 12, 1999, President Clinton signed Rush's bill, the Nursing Relief for Disadvantaged Areas Act of 1999, into public law. The law temporarily addressed the nursing shortage by providing nonimmigrant visas for qualified foreign nurses in the Englewood area of Chicago.

On October 17, 2000, Congress passed the Urban Asthma Reduction Act of 1999. This bill incorporated parts of Congressman Rush's original bill into the Children's Health Act of 2000, which eventually became Public Law No. 106-310. This law amends the Preventive Health & Health Services Block Grant program and includes an integrated approach to vermin management.

Early in his first term, Congressman Rush enjoyed unparalleled success when President Clinton signed into law the Community

Development and Regulatory Act, a landmark community banking bill that was based largely on a plan Rush first introduced in Congress.

Always keeping his constituents' issues in mind, Congressman Rush initiated the Chicago Partnership for the Earned Income Tax Credit, an ongoing program designed to help thousands of low-income working Chicagoans receive federal tax credits.

Congressman Rush has brought close to $2 billion of federal funding to the First Congressional District of Illinois since his election as well as a $1 million federal grant from the U.S. Office of Naval Research to the Illinois Institute of Technology. This grant will help to develop easier and faster ways to assess the presence of chemical and biological agents and will be the key to stronger homeland security and to the safety of U.S. troops all over the world.

NOTES

1. Dingell, J. D. (1996, June 10). Remarks from a speech presented to the Computer and Communications Industry Association. Retrieved January 25, 2006, from http://www.house.gov/commerce_democrats/comdem/press/104rm7.htm.

2. Rush, B. (n.d.). *Accomplishments of Bobby L. Rush*. Retrieved January 25, 2006, from http://www.dixontech.com/rush/bio.htm#bio.

3. Office of Congressman Bobby Rush. (2003, May 9). *U.S. Rep. Bobby Rush introduces Telecommunications Ownership Diversification Act of 2003*. Retrieved January 25, 2006 http://www.house.gov/apps/list/press/il01_rush/pr_030509_hr2044.html.

4. Office of Congressman Bobby Rush. (2003, June 5). *U.S. Rep. Bobby Rush announces minority cable and telecommunications supplier program*. Retrieved January 25, 2006, from http://www.house.gov/apps/list/press/il01_rush/pr_030605_minoritycable.html.

5. Congress of the United States. (1998, June 5). Rush fights to keep national Internet program funded. *Tech Law Journal*. Retrieved January 25, 2006, from http://www.techlawjournal.com/agencies/slc/80605rush.htm.

6. Gross, G. (2004, June 17). Internet promotion program abused. *PC World*. Retrieved January 25, 2006, from http://www.pcworld.com/news/article/0,aid,116563,00.asp.

7. Rockefeller, J., Snowe, O., Rush, B., & Blumenauer, E. (n.d.). Transcript of press conference. *Tech Law Journal*. Retrieved January 25, 2006, from http://www.techlawjournal.com/agencies/slc/80605pc.htm.

8. On the Issues. (n.d.). *Bobby Rush on technology*. Retrieved January 25, 2006, from http://www.issues2000.org/IL/Bobby_Rush_Technology.htm.

9. Office of Congressman Bobby Rush. (2003, November 24). *Bobby L. Rush Center for Community Technology gets boost with $1 million grant from SBC Foundation.* Retrieved January 25, 2006, from http://www.house.gov/apps/list/press/il01_rush/pr_031121.html.

10. Rush, B. L. (n.d.). *About Congressman Bobby L. Rush.* Retrieved January 25, 2006, from http://www.house.gov/rush/bio.shtml.

Chapter 8

Edolphus Towns

U.S. Representative, Tenth Congressional District, New York

BRINGING ECONOMIC BENEFITS OF TECHNOLOGY TO THE BLACK COMMUNITY

The Telecommunications Act of 1996 requires the Federal Communications Commission (FCC) to identify and eliminate "market entry barriers for entrepreneurs and other small businesses in the provision and ownership of telecommunications services and information services." In carrying out this mandate, the commission must "promote the policies and purposes of this Act favoring diversity of media voices, vigorous economic competition, technological advancement, and promotion of the public interest, convenience and necessity." The FCC, therefore, created a Telecommunications Development Fund (TDF) to promote access to capital for small businesses in the telecommunications industry, to stimulate the development of new technologies, and to support the delivery of universal service and telecommunications services to underserved rural and urban areas.[1,2] When former FCC chair Reed

Hundt appointed a seven-member board of directors to administer the fund, he stated:

Their expertise will help provide funding for small businesses, create jobs and promote technological innovation in the telecommunications industry ... I commend congressional leadership, and in particular Congressman Edolphus Towns of New York, who sponsored the amendment which created the Fund, for their creativity and vision.[3]

Towns wrote the TDF legislation into the 1996 telecommunications law as one of his many efforts to make sure that all Americans could participate in the economic benefits of the Information Revolution. TDF was established to help entrepreneurs with access to capital and consists of two organizations[4,5]: a venture capital fund focused on making direct investments in promising entrepreneurs and companies focused on the communications sector; and a separate nonprofit organization—Outreach—that targets potential and aspiring entrepreneurs and provides education and training in preparation for raising institutional capital for their companies. TDF focuses on investments in digital television and high definition technology and services, wireless technology and services, public safety, urban and rural communications, security, broadband access, and Internet protocol services. TDF manages $50 million and makes investments up to $2.5 million. In addition to the traditional services provided by a venture capital fund, TDF has provided financial advice and training through its numerous entrepreneurial outreach activities. Since 2000, TDF has participated in more than 500 events, reaching more than 25,000 entrepreneurs in 23 states.

As a member of the Telecommunications and Internet Subcommittee of the House Energy and Commerce Committee, Congressman Towns has promoted several legislative initiatives to ensure that technological innovations are developed and shared by all communities. In 2003, he introduced the Telecommunications Development Fund Improvement Act, which would make it easier to offer loans to start up technology and telecom companies in underserved areas. "This would spur minority entrepreneurship in inner cities, and could eventually lead to new, minority-owned technology businesses in our own neighborhoods." This legislation has been included as part of a larger bill that has already passed the Telecommunication and Internet Subcommittee and has been forwarded to the full House Energy and Commerce Committee.

In the 107th Congress, Towns authored the Internet Freedom and Broadband Deployment Act, which would ensure that inner cities and other underserved areas have access to high-speed Internet services. Bridging the digital divide is essential to ensuring that minority-owned small business can flourish and that inner city schools can provide 21st-century technology for students.

CLOSING TECHNOLOGY GAPS AT HISTORICALLY BLACK COLLEGES AND UNIVERSITIES

In the U.S. Congress, Towns has been an ardent fighter for African Americans' participation in the Information Revolution. He believes that the key is providing historically Black colleges and universities (HBCUs) with the technological resources that they need to make their graduates competitive in the future information society in America[6,7]: "We need to make sure that our students graduating from HBCUs have the same opportunities and resources as students from other public or private universities. If we do not act or continue to push for additional resources, our students will be at a disadvantage in the marketplace.[8] Research indicates that two out of five public HBCUs are in urgent need of upgrades to their technological infrastructure and on only one out of 45 campuses do more than 75 percent of students own computers. In the U.S. House of Representatives in 2001, Towns introduced the NTIA Digital Network Technology Program Act, which would have established a digital network technologies program to award grants, contracts, or cooperative agreements to institutions to provide educational instruction in digital network technologies. The assistance would be targeted for institutions that serve population groups who have not fully participated in the technological revolution such as African Americans and other minorities. Because the first bill never became law, however, more recently Towns cosponsored the Minority Serving Institution Digital and Wireless Technology Opportunity Act.

This bill will give our students attending HBCUs and other Minority Serving Institutions the help they need to leap into the 21st century with both feet solidly on the ground. We must ensure that students attending these places of higher education have access to the technological training and skills needed to be competitive in today's workforce.

The legislation would provide up to $250 million each year to help HBCUs and other minority-serving institutions to acquire digital network technology as well as wireless technology and infrastructure to develop and provide educational services to students, faculty, and staff. Additionally, the grants could be used for equipment upgrades, technology training, and computer hardware or software acquisition.

In the meantime, while the new bill is making its way through Congress, Towns secured $10 million for Thurgood Marshall Program funds to upgrade the technology infrastructure at Black colleges.[9] "While they certainly have a great tradition and history, we need to ensure that the future on HBCU campuses is just as bright," Towns said. "The [Thurgood Marshall Scholarship Fund] was established in 1987 to carry on Justice Marshall's legacy of equal access to higher education by supporting exceptional merit scholars attending HBCUs."

BIOGRAPHY

Towns was born in Chadbourn, Columbus County, NC, on July 21, 1934. He graduated from West Side High School in Chadbourn in 1952, received his Bachelor of Science degree from North Carolina Agricultural and Technical State University, Greensboro, in 1956, and served in the U.S. Army from 1956 to 1958. He was awarded a Master of Social Work degree from Adelphi University in 1973.

Towns began his political career as deputy president of the borough of Brooklyn, NY, from 1976 to 1982, the first African American to serve in that position.[10] Additionally, he and his son, New York State Assemblyman Darryl Towns, became the first African American father–son tandem to serve simultaneously in public office in New York State.

Towns's varied professional background includes assignments as an administrator at Beth Israel Medical Center, a professor at New York's Medgar Evers College and Fordham University, and a teacher in the New York City public school system. He is currently serving his twelfth term in the U.S. House of Representatives. He represents the Tenth Congressional District of Brooklyn, NY, encompassing the neighborhoods of East New York, Canarsie, Brownsville, Bedford–Stuyvesant, Cypress Hills, Clinton Hill, Mill Basin, Midwood, downtown Brooklyn, and Boreum Hill, as well as parts of Fort Greene and Williamsburg.

Towns is a member of the exclusive Energy and Commerce Committee, where he is on the Commerce, Trade, and Consumer Protection Subcommittee, the Health Subcommittee, and the Telecommunications and the Internet Subcommittee. Through his committee appointments, Representative Towns has worked to enhance consumers' privacy protections on the Internet, develop innovative initiatives to reduce asthma, and bridge the digital divide. He also serves on the Government Reform Committee's Subcommittee on Government Efficiency and Financial Management, where he is the ranking member.

Throughout his tenure in Congress, Towns's legislative work in education, telecommunications, health care, financial services, and the environment has earned him numerous awards. Some of his legislative successes include the Student Right to Know Act, a law to mandate the reporting of student-athlete graduation rates, new bilingual education programs for the gifted and talented, teacher training and special education, enhanced Medicare reimbursement rates for midlevel practitioners, a federal funding base for poison control centers, new standards for the inclusion of children in clinical trials, and creation of the TDF to provide capital for small and minority telecommunications businesses.

In the environmental area, Towns continues to be committed to protecting national parks and creating open space throughout Brooklyn, including the Brooklyn Bridge Park project, of which he was an original incorporator. He has also worked to preserve and restore ecologically sensitive estuaries and coastal areas. In addition, the National Audubon Society recognized the congressman for his leadership in securing federal funds for restoration activities in Prospect Park. Representative Towns has brought important economic development projects to the Tenth Congressional District as well.

Towns, an ordained Baptist minister, is married to the former Gwendolyn Forbes, and they reside in the Cypress Hills section of Brooklyn. They have two children, Darryl and Deidra, and five grandchildren, Kiara, Jasmine, Kristian, Dale, and Trinity. The congressman also serves as a surrogate father to his nephews Jason and Jereme Towns.

NOTES

1. Carlson, C. (1997, May 19). TDF loan reserve grows. *Wireless Week.* Retrieved January 26, 2006, from http://www.wirelessweek.com/article/CA4944.html?spacedesc=.

2. Williams, B. (2003, June 18). *The FCC's strange non-profit.* Retrieved January 26, 2006, from The Center for Public Integrity Web site: http://www.publicintegrity.org/telecom/report.aspx?aid=31.

3. Federal Communications Commission. (1996, October 1). *FCC Chairman Hundt appoints private sector members to the Telecommunications Development Fund board.* Retrieved January 26, 2006, from http://www.benton.org/publibrary/policy/TDF/newmems.html.

4. TDF. (n.d.). *About TDF.* Retrieved January 27, 2006, from http://www.tdfund.com/.

5. Donovan, G. (2003, October 11). *BEDC presents "The venture capital landscape: Does equity capital fit my business?"* Retrieved January 26, 2006, from the Brooklyn Economic Development Corporation Web site: http://www.bedc.org/pressrelease/pr_10-11-02_ven.htm.

6. U.S. Department of Commerce. (2000, October). *Historically Black colleges and universities: An assessment of networking and connectivity.* Retrieved January 26, 2006, from http://search.ntia.doc.gov/nafeo.pdf.

7. Hurd, H. (2000, November 9). Majority of HBCUs "keeping pace" with technology. *Black Issues in Higher Education.* Retrieved May 10, 2006, from http://www.diverseeducation.com/cgi-bin/artman/exec/view.cgi?archive=2&num=977.

8. U.S. Congress. (2005, February 17). *Towns announces plan to reintroduce bill providing technology funding for minority serving institutions.* Retrieved January 27, 2006, from http://www.house.gov/apps/list/press/ny10_towns/prhbcu.html.

9. U.S. Congress. (2004, December 13). *Towns secures $10 million for Thurgood Marshall program funds to upgrade technology infrastructure of Black colleges.* Retrieved January 27, 2006, from http://www.house.gov/apps/list/press/ny10_towns/prtmsf.html.

10. Office of Congressman Edolphus Towns. (n.d.). *Biography.* Retrieved January 26, 2006, from http://www.house.gov/towns/bio.shtm.

Chapter 9

Albert R. Wynn

U.S. Representative, Fourth Congressional District, Maryland

OVERHAULING POLICY FOR THE INFORMATION AGE

The Telecommunication Act of 1996 paved the way for unprecedented expansion of the information infrastructure in America, but it was insufficient to regulate all of the changes that have emerged over the past decade.[1–4] Congressman Joe Barton, chair of the House Committee on Energy and Commerce, maintains that the 1996 act addressed telecommunications competition but could not have "foreseen the magnitude of the challenges and opportunities that the Internet age has presented."[5] Barton added that updating the bill is one of his top priorities for fall 2006: "New services shouldn't be hamstrung by old thinking and outdated regulations. We need a fresh new approach that will encourage Internet providers to expand and improve broadband networks, spur growth in the technology sector and develop cutting-edge services for consumers."

When Barton made his statement, Congressman Albert R. Wynn was already taking the lead in overhauling the law that served for a decade as the blueprint for the Information Revolution in America at the close of the 20th century. On June 30, 2005, Wynn and U.S. Representative Marsha Blackburn introduced the Video Choice Act of 2005, one of the first pieces of legislation that would move the Congress toward reform of the 1996 telecommunications law.[6] Wynn's legislation would prohibit local governments from asserting franchise agreements over traditional telephone providers offering competitive video services. At the time, the law required that companies interested in offering video service negotiate an individual agreement with each local franchising authority. This mandate served as a barrier to competition and prevented new technologies from entering the marketplace.

The Video Choice Act of 2005 streamlined the franchising process for new entrants but still required that providers pay the same franchise fees that incumbent cable operators pay. Like current cable operators, they would also have to make government and education channels available. As of this writing, the bill has been referred to the House Committee on Energy and Commerce and has four cosponsors. A companion measure, S. 1349, was introduced in the Senate by Gordon Smith (R-OR) and John D. Rockefeller (D-WV). S. 1349 has been referred to the Senate Commerce Committee and has no cosponsors.

American consumers are paying higher television service rates today because of the hoops we require new providers to jump through. We need to bring these outdated regulations into the twenty-first century. You cannot expect the current system to meet the expectations of modern consumers who are used to choice and competition in virtually every area of daily life. I am pleased to join Congressman Wynn in this effort, and look forward to making the case for our legislation.

REFORMING INTERNET POLICY

Wynn serves on the House Committee on Energy and Commerce, where he is a member of the Subcommittee on Telecommunications and the Internet. The Video Choice Act was not Wynn's first attempt to bring the information laws and policies into the twenty-first century. He also cosponsored the Internet Freedom and Broadband Deployment Act of 2001.[7] This legislation would spur the growth of high-speed Internet service, or broadband, to all areas of the country. This legislation would allow the Bell companies, such as Verizon, to enter the long-distance market for the purpose of carrying Internet data, a practice currently prohibited under law. With the removal of these barriers, Congressman Wynn expects broadband to be deployed in more areas more quickly and the price for its service to drop as the Bell companies become real competitors to cable.

At the press conference to announce the legislation, Wynn stated, "This bill is a much needed economic stimulus measure. It will speed our nation's broadband deployment and promote growth in our nation's technology sectors. This legislation is important to closing the digital divide that exists in many rural and urban communities. It is sound policy and I look forward to seeing this piece of legislation voted on and passed."

In the coming months and years, a new communications policy will be needed to keep pace with changes in technology and consumer services. Wynn's initiatives have helped set the stage for a new set of telecommunications policies as the information revolution in America continues to unfold.

PROVIDING TECHNOLOGY TO AFRICAN AMERICANS

Wynn, like his colleagues in the Congressional Black Caucus (CBC), recognizes that policies are needed to close technology gaps in the African American community.[8] He has supported the position of the CBC on technology issues and the role of African Americans. The CBC believes that training is the key to African Americans obtaining high-tech jobs. Wynn has been focused on closing the "digital divide" and moving toward digital empowerment for all Americans.

In 2000, Wynn joined his colleagues in the House and the Senate and introduced the National Digital Empowerment Act to train African American children to be computer literate by the time they reach the eighth grade. Wynn continues to support this legislation and policy, which ensure that African American and all the nation's children have access to technology and the opportunities it affords.

BIOGRAPHY

Wynn was born in Philadelphia, PA, and graduated from DuVal High School, Lanham, MD, in 1969.[9] He received his Bachelor of Science degree in political science from the University of Pittsburgh in 1973. After a year of graduate study in public administration at Howard

University, Wynn entered Georgetown University and earned his law degree in 1977. Upon graduation, he became director of the Prince George's County Consumer Protection Commission.

In 1982, he started the law office of Albert R. Wynn and Associates and was elected to the Maryland legislature, where he served a decade first as a member of the House of Delegates and later in the Maryland Senate.

Wynn represents the Fourth Congressional District of Maryland, which includes parts of Prince George's and Montgomery Counties. He defines his mission in Congress as helping to expand economic opportunity for all Americans. He is a member of the Democratic Message Group and a deputy democratic whip. Wynn also chairs the CBC Task Force on Campaign Finance Reform and the Caucus Minority Business Task Force. In addition to his efforts on information and telecommunications policy reform, Congressman Wynn is a known advocate for federal employees and small business development. Throughout his tenure in Congress, Wynn has fought to protect the salaries and benefits of federal employees. He also has led efforts to end discrimination in the federal workforce. Wynn has cosponsored important legislation on increasing the minimum wage, job training, and increasing access to child care.

During the 105th Congress, Wynn successfully passed legislation to improve federal contracting opportunities for small and minority businesses. As a result of his many efforts on behalf of small businesses, he is a two-time recipient of the Small Business Administration's Administrator's Leadership Award. In his community, Wynn sponsors an annual job fair, a federal procurement fair/business expo, a college financial aid workshop, and a student leadership workshop. He also coordinates food distributions for the less fortunate every Thanksgiving and Christmas.

Wynn is a member of Kappa Alpha Psi Fraternity, Inc., and attends Maple Springs Baptist Church. He is married to Gaines Clore Wynn, an artist and art educator. Together, they have a blended family of two daughters, Meredith and Gabrielle. They are also the proud grandparents of Kaden Nicholas born in January 2004.

NOTES

1. Wexler, C. V. (2005, May 9). *The fallout from the Telecommunications Act of 1996: Unintended consequences and lessons learned.* Retrieved January 29, 2006, from the Common Cause Education Fund Web

site: http://www.commoncause.org/atf/cf/%7bfb3c17e2-cdd1-4df6-92be-bd 4429893665%7d/fallout_from_the_telecomm_act_5-9-05.PDF.

2. Clark, D. (2005, December 8). *Barton abandons bid to vote on Telecom bill next week.* Retrieved January 27, 2006, from the National Journal Web site: http://www.njtelecomupdate.com/lenya/telco/live/tb-SADO1134082921701. html.

3. CTCNet. (2005, November 15). *So, when's the Telecommunications Act coming?* Retrieved January 27, 2006, from the Digital Access Web site: http://www.digitalaccess.org/ctcnet.htm.

4. Gross, G. (2004, May 19). Can convergence thrive under old laws? *PC World.* Retrieved January 27, 2006, from http://www.pcworld.com/ resource/printable/article/0,aid,116196,00.asp#.

5. Telecom Web. (2005, September 19). *In the House: Telecom-reform "discussion draft" surfaces.* Retrieved January 30, 2006, from http://www. telecomweb.com/news/tpr/12836.html.

6. Wynn, A. (n.d.). *Blackburn, Wynn introduce telecom reform legislation.* Retrieved January 27, 2006, from http://wynn.house.gov/issues2. cfm?id=10802.

7. Wynn, A. (2001, December 5). *Wynn joins colleagues in support of Tauzin-Dingell.* Retrieved January 30, 2006, http://wynn.house.gov/issues2. cfm?id=3118.

8. On the Issues. (n.d.). *Albert Wynn on technology.* Retrieved January 29, 2006, from http://www.issues2000.org/House/Albert_Wynn_Technology. htm.

9. Office of Congressman Albert Wynn. (n.d.). *Biography.* Retrieved January 30, 2006, from http://wynn.house.gov/display2.cfm?id=3021& type=Hot%20Topics.

Chapter 10

William E. Kennard

Former Chairman,
Federal
Communications
Commission

BEING FIRST AT THE FEDERAL COMMUNICATIONS COMMISSION

The Federal Communications Commission (FCC) is the government agency charged with ensuring that the goals of the historic Telecommunications Act of 1996 are achieved. In 1997, former President Bill Clinton appointed William E. Kennard to the chairmanship of the FCC.[1] Kennard was not only the first African American to head the commission, but the first chairman of any race to be the chief regulator of the unprecedented changes that were taking place in the American communication and information technology industries at the dawn of the 21st century.[2–4] Serving as chairman from 1997 to 2001, Kennard implemented policies that helped to create an explosion of new wireless phones, bring the Internet to a majority of American households, and make digital-age technologies more available to schools, libraries, low-income Americans, and people with disabilities.

The FCC's key role in government is to examine how industry activities and changes will affect the public. When Kennard took office, the Information Revolution brought more attention to the FCC than ever before. Kennard was responsible for overseeing proposals for industry giants to join together to form the megacorporations of an emerging communications marketplace. As chairman of the commission, he shaped the outcome of the most significant communications mergers in history, including AOL and Time Warner, Worldcom and MCI, CBS and Viacom, Verizon and GTE, and SBC and Ameritech.[5-8] The AOL Time Warner merger was touted as the largest in the industry history at the time that it was approved by the FCC. It also epitomized the vision of the national information infrastructure because it brought together several companies that could provide members of the American public with Internet service and cable television as well as movies, newspapers, magazines, and other information products and services.

CLOSING THE DIGITAL DIVIDE: FIGHTING FOR THE E-RATE

Kennard was not only an advocate of competition and growth in the telecommunications industries but an advocate for people at risk of being stranded on the wrong side of the digital divide. He aggressively implemented the FCC's Education Rate (E-Rate) program by investing more than $6 billion to bring the Internet to 95 percent of K–12 schools and 58,000 libraries across the nation.[9-12] In touting the accomplishments of the E-Rate program, Kennard said that the program was a success in connecting all children—rich and poor— to the Internet. By the end of 1999, 95 percent of America's schools were connected to the Internet as a result of this program. When the FCC rolled out the E-Rate program, it targeted schools and libraries with the least connections: those that serve poor and rural neighborhoods. In the program's first two years, more than 75 percent of all public schools and districts applied for funding, more than 50 percent of all public libraries participated, and more than 5,000 private schools sought funding.

During Kennard's administration, the FCC also dramatically expanded access to communications technologies for people with disabilities.[13] The FCC adopted policies to increase telephone service to rural areas, especially for Native Americans living on tribal lands. Kennard also reached out to create more ownership and employment opportunities for women and minorities in the mass media and

communications industries. His policy initiatives to increase employment of African Americans and other minorities were eventually
overturned by the courts.[14-16]

AFRICAN AMERICANS AND THE DIGITAL AGE

Kennard expressed his views on how African Americans must
approach the digital age in presentations at meetings of Black institutions and organizations across the country.[17,18] Speaking at the
commencement ceremony at Howard University in Washington, DC,
in 2000, he said:

Much has been given to you. I call you Generation D, the digital generation.
You will graduate into a world where the Internet will give you instantaneous access to global markets; where you can use a device that you will hold
in the palm of your hand to access more information than is contained in
the Howard University library. And I know you will go forward to invent
even greater technologies and with them you will achieve what we cannot
even imagine today. At the dawn of the last century, W. E. B. Du Bois said,
'The problem of the 20th century is the problem of the color line.' At the
dawn of this century, our challenge is to make sure that the color line does
not determine who is on-line.

Kennard believes that African American college graduates must
use determination to lead the Black community and the nation to
where it should be. He said that the civil rights challenge for the next
century is to make sure that African Americans, and all Americans,
share in the benefits of the Information Age:

The long term solution is not new. It's as old as Brown v. Board of Education. We must ensure racial equality in education. But the new twist is that
technology is dramatically transforming education in this society and, if we
don't make sure that all kids have equality of access to technology, the digital divide will only widen.

Kennard feels that this challenge has three components: accessing
technology, gaining employment in communications and information technology, and owning communications and information technology companies. He feels that government can and should play a
role in fostering opportunities in these three areas.

BIOGRAPHY

Kennard was born in Los Angeles, CA. He graduated Phi Beta Kappa
from Stanford University in 1978 and received his law degree from

Yale Law School in 1981. He has received honorary degrees from Howard University, Gallaudet University, and Long Island University.

Before joining the FCC, from 1982 to 1993 Kennard was a partner and member of the board of directors of the Washington, DC, law firm of Verner, Liipfert, Bernhard, McPherson & Hand. He specialized in communications law, with an emphasis on regulatory and transactional matters for communications companies.[19]

In the 1980s he served on the FCC's Advisory Committee on Minority Ownership in Broadcasting. Kennard is a member of the District of Columbia and California bars and has served as treasurer, secretary, and assistant secretary of the Federal Communications Bar Association. For 3½ years before becoming the chairman of the FCC, Kennard served as the agency's general counsel and as a practicing attorney was involved in a broad range of communications issues. As the commission's chief legal officer, Kennard was responsible for advising the commission on all matters involving the interpretation and application of the Communications Act of 1934. The general counsel also serves as the commission's legal representative in all litigation involving the commission. As FCC general counsel, Kennard served as the commission's principal legal advisor and represented the commission in court.

Kennard joined The Carlyle Group in May 2001 as a managing director in the Global Telecommunications and Media Group. Based in Washington, DC, Kennard has played key roles in the investments in Dex Media, Inc., and Casema Holding BV and the acquisition of Hawaii Telcom. He is a member of the boards of directors of Nextel Communications, Inc., The New York Times Company, Dex Media, Inc., and eAccess, Ltd. He is married to Deborah Diane Kennedy of Greenville, SC. She is managing counsel at Mobil Corporation.

NOTES

1. Mills, M. (1997, July 25). Kennard is choice for FCC chief. *The Washington Post*. Retrieved January 24, 2006, from http://pqasb. pqarchiver.com/washingtonpost/search.html/?nav=left.

2. Borland, J., & Grice, C. (1999, October 11). *Holding the keys to the telecom kingdom*. Retrieved January 24, 2006, from the CNet News Web site: http://news.com.com/2009-1023-231063.html.

3. Kennard, W. E. (2001, January 12). *Outgoing Federal Communications Commission Chairman William Kennard discusses the AOL-Time Warner*

merger. Retrieved January 24, 2006, from the PBS Web site: http://www.pbs.org/newshour/bb/business/jan-june01/kennard_1-12.html.

4. Semilof, M. (2000, November 6). *The rule maker: William Kennard*. Retrieved January 24, 2006, from the CRN Web site: http://www.crn.com/sections/special/top25/top25_00.jhtml;jsessionid=CR3GEPGFSD1FOQSNDBGCKH0CJUMEKJVN?articleId=188121656_requestid=1615439.

5. Ness, S. (1998, July 24). *Mergers and consolidation in the telecommunications industry*. Retrieved May 12, 2006, from http://www.fcc.gov/Speeches/Ness/States/stsn820.html

6. Borland, J. (1999, December 29). *Mergers: How big is big enough?* Retrieved January 24, 2006, from the CNET News Web site: http://news.com.com/Mergers+How+big+is+big+enough/2100-1033_3-234978.html.

7. (2001, January). The FCC's Kennard: "Create as much competition as you can." *BusinessWeek Online*. Retrieved June 27, 2006, from http://www.businessweek.com/bwdaily/dnflash/jan2001/nf2001015_884.htm.

8. Hu, J. (2000, December 18). *Gates urges regulators to address instant messaging*. Retrieved January 24, 2006, from the CNet News web site: http://news.com.com/Gates+urges+regulators+to+address+instant+messaging/2100-1023_3-250008.html.

9. Fusco, P. (2000, April 14). *FCC distributing first wave of Y2K's $2 billion E-Rate funding*. Retrieved January 24, 2006, from ISP-Planet Web site: http://www.isp-planet.com/news/e-rate_distribution.html.

10. Kennard, W. E. (2000, January 14). *E Rate: A success story*. Speech presented at the Educational Technology Leadership Conference, Washington, DC.

11. Warner, E. (1998, June 15). Kennard: Reduce E-Rate subsidy. *Wirelessweek*. Retrieved January 24, 2006, from http://www.wirelessweek.com/index.asp?layout=articlePrint&articleID=CA4318.

12. "Kennard asks NAACP to support E-Rate." (1998, July 15). *Tech Law Journal*. Retrieved May 12, 2006, from http://www.techlawjournal.com/telecom/80715wk.htm.

13. Kennard, W. E. (1999, November 15). *The new frontier for civil rights in the twenty first century*. Speech presented to the President's Committee on Employment of Persons with Disabilities, Washington, DC.

14. Kennard, W. E. (1998, August 3). *Remarks*. Speech presented to the meeting of the National Urban League, Philadelphia.

15. Kennard, W. E. (1998, December 2). *Mastering opportunity*. Speech presented to the National Black Media Coalition, Washington, DC.

16. Labaton, S. (2001, January 17). Court rules agency erred on mandate for minorities. *New York Times*. Retrieved January 25, 2006, from http://select.nytimes.com/gst/abstract.html?res=FB0D12F63B590C748DDDA80894D9404482&n=Top%2fReference%2fTimes%20Topics%2fPeople%2fK%2fKennard%2c%20William%20E%2e.

17. Kennard, W. E. (1998, July 13). *Thinking ahead*. Speech presented at the NAACP Annual Convention Telecommunications Forum, Atlanta.

18. Kennard, W. E. (2000, May 13). *The challenge to Generation D: Beyond the color line*. Commencement address presented at Howard University, Washington, DC.

19. Federal Communications Commission. (n.d.). *Biography of William E. Kennard*. Retrieved January 25, 2006, from http://www.fcc.gov/commissioners/previous/kennard/biography.html.

Chapter 11

Michael K. Powell

Former Chairman,
Federal
Communications
Commission

MANAGING THE DIGITAL BROADBAND MIGRATION

When President George Bush appointed Michael K. Powell to the chair of the Federal Communications Commission (FCC) in 2001, the head of the congressional committee that oversees the nation's communications systems congratulated him on his new position.[1] Congressman W. J. Tauzin, chairman of the House Committee on Energy and Commerce, told Powell, "I look forward to working with you on a panoply of exciting issues during your tenure. I am deeply pleased that we share a vision of an FCC operating in an efficient and expeditious manner to, among other things, faithfully implement the Telecommunications Act of 1996. However, despite the fact that the Act recently celebrated its fifth birthday, many issues remain unresolved by the Commission."

Picking up where William Kennard left off, Powell began to resolve the communications challenges facing a nation in the middle of an ongoing Information Revolution. As the head of the FCC,

Powell became the regulatory overseer of the industries that made up the national information infrastructure, including Internet, cable, satellite, wireless, television, and radio. These enterprises at that time had more than $1 trillion in annual sales.[2]

Powell moved to match regulatory polices with the rapid development and spread of information and communication technology. His main aim was to implement a hands-off approach to regulation so that the industries could grow and thrive. Powell established the agenda for regulation in the age of new media. His regulatory schematic was based on a concept he called "digital broadband migration."[3-5] He used this term because he realized that breakthroughs in technology were driving an exodus from existing analog platforms to digital architectures. He fought for the development of policies that would facilitate this electronic migration in areas such as broadband deployment, telephone competition, electronic media regulation, homeland security, and allocation of the airwaves for various uses.

In deployment of broadband services, Powell sought to foster universal access in all sectors, including telephone, cable, satellite, and Internet. He moved to lift restrictions to building new networks. Where phone competition was concerned, Powell sought to reduce restrictions in order for local upstart companies to compete with larger companies. He also attempted to increase the number of electronic media that owners could control at one time. In homeland security, he encouraged policies that would help the nation secure its communications systems in a post-9/11 environment. Powell also sought ways to increase the amount of the airwaves that wireless companies could use to provide services to consumers.

CHANGING THE RULES OF THE GAME

Powell received much national attention when he attempted to promulgate new media ownership policies that would have allowed the television networks to own a few more stations, tightened national radio ownership rules, and let one company own the largest newspaper and television station in almost every city.[6,7] These policy proposals received widespread reaction from the public. Almost all of them opposed the weakening of the nation's media ownership regulations. A court that said the commission had failed to justify the ruling later overturned the rules.

Despite his attempt to have a deregulatory agenda at the FCC, Powell's tenure will probably be most remembered for the Super Bowl halftime show controversy in which pop singer Janet Jackson exposed a bare nipple on live-broadcast television. This high-profile incident increased public attention toward the FCC's enforcement of indecency rules that had already stepped up after Bono's use of an expletive on live television.[8–10] Howard Stern and other lesser known shock jocks felt the sting of record fines, and both the U.S. House of Representatives and the Senate separately approved legislation significantly increasing the fines for indecency that could be levied against stations. Although the legislation was not ultimately enacted, the climate in Washington became so gray that several television stations across the country declined to air "Saving Private Ryan" on Veterans Day for fear of FCC fines.

AFRICAN AMERICANS AND THE INFORMATION AGE

Although Powell spent a great deal of time focusing on the digital revolution during his administration, his comments on the digital divide were often criticized:[11,12]

The term sometimes is dangerous in the sense that it suggests that the minute a new and innovative technology comes to market there is a divide unless it's equitably distributed among every part of the society. Even though the wealthy will be the first to afford new technologies such as digital television sets or computers when they come to market, that doesn't necessarily translate to a divide. If so, I think there is a Mercedes divide. I'd like to have one.

Nevertheless, Powell was concerned about the place of African Americans and other minorities in the Information Revolution. Powell believes that in the Information Age African Americans need a different approach to success than that used in the civil rights era. African Americans should pursue principles that level the playing field for all participants, encourage private sector initiatives, jettison the rationales of the past, include economics-based initiatives, and create win–win situations.

In 2003, Powell put some of his thinking about the empowerment of African Americans in the Information Age into action. Speaking at the American Bar Association Summit, he emphasized that diversity is a business imperative and pointed out that by 2008 African Americans' buying power would reach $921 billion or 8.7 percent of the nation's buying power.[13] Moreover, Powell said that the communications sector needed to tap the diversity of the American public if it was going to continue to provide services needed by the American people. To this end, he established the Federal Advisory Committee on Diversity for Communication in the Digital Age. The Committee has four responsibilities: (1) developing strategies that will enhance participation by minorities and women in telecommunications and related-industry transactions, including timely knowledge of potential transactions and access to the necessary capital; (2) developing strategies to increase educational training for minorities and women that facilitates opportunities in upper level management and ownership; (3) developing strategies to enhance participation and ownership by minorities and women in the newly developing industries based on new technologies; and (4) gathering the information and performing the analyses necessary for meeting the committee's responsibilities:

The focus of this particular Advisory Committee, and indeed the imperative for all companies involved in the Information Revolution, is to look for goals of diversity flow not to promote just minority employment in communications companies but minority advancement within those companies and minority ownership of those companies. Moreover, this Committee should look at all of those issues not just for media companies but for all telecommunications and other companies that the FCC oversees.

Powell said that he hoped that his committee would help to convince the American communications industry that diversity is a business imperative that will differentiate marketplace winners from marketplace losers.

BIOGRAPHY

Powell was born in Birmingham, AL, in 1963,[14] the year of lunch counter sit-ins, Dr. Martin Luther King's "Letter from Birmingham Jail," and the murder of four little girls in church. It was also the year that Dr. King stood on the steps of The Lincoln Memorial in Washington, DC, and declared "I have a dream."

Powell is the son of Colin Powell, who, before becoming secretary of state, was a general in the U.S. Army and chairman of the joint chiefs of staff. The younger Powell eventually followed in his famous father's footsteps and became a soldier. The son was an armored cavalry officer in the U.S. Army stationed in Amberg, Germany, but was unable to serve after sustaining severe injuries during a training mission in 1987. After initial attention from German emergency room doctors, Powell was flown to Washington, DC, and spent a year in recovery at Walter Reed Army Medical Center. To this day, his spine is still fused at its base, forcing him to walk with a slight forward pitch. After his rehabilitation, he served as an expert advisor to the secretary of defense.

Michael Powell later received a Juris Doctor degree from Georgetown University Law Center and clerked for the U.S. Court of Appeals. He then worked for 1½ years as a private attorney in the Washington, DC, office of O'Melveny & Myers, a Los Angeles-based firm. In addition, Powell served as chief of staff in the Antitrust Division of the U.S. Department of Justice for 1 year. In that capacity, he advised the assistant attorney general on substantive antitrust matters, including policy development, criminal and civil investigations, and mergers.

A Republican, Powell was nominated by President William J. Clinton on July 31, 1997, and was confirmed by the U.S. Senate on October 28, 1997. In November 1997, Powell was sworn in as a member of the commission. He was designated chairman by President Bush on January 22, 2001. In addition to his normal duties, Mr. Powell served as the FCC's defense chairman and was responsible for overseeing all national security emergency preparedness functions for the commission. He also served as the FCC representative to the President's Council on Year 2000 Conversion, established by President Clinton on February 4, 1998, to address the Year 2000 computer problem. After leaving the FCC, Powell joined the private equity firm Providence Equity Partners in Providence, RI. As a senior advisor, he advises the firm on technological and regulatory issues, including investment opportunities in the private equity field.

NOTES

1. Tauzin, W. J. (2001, February 15). *Issues pertaining to reciprocal compensation.* Retrieved May 15, from http://energycommerce.house.gov/107/letters/02152001_55.htm.

2. Pulley, B. (2002, April 29). *Commander of the airwaves.* Retrieved May 15, from the Forbes Web site: http://www.forbes.com/archive/forbes/2002/0429/078.html;jsessionid=sQNp1yyMTA8ARA64?token=MTUgTWF5IDIwMDYgMTY6Mzg6MjYgKzAwMDA%3D.

3. Powell, M. K. (2004, January 14). *The age of personal communications power to the people.* Speech presented to the National Press Club, Washington, DC.

4. Powell, M. K. (2002, October 30). *Broadband migration III: New directions in wireless policy.* Speech presented to the Silicon Flatirons Telecommunications Program, University of Colorado at Boulder.

5. Powell, M. K. (2001, October 30). *Digital broadband migration.* Speech presented at the FCC Press Conference, Washington, DC.

6. Federal Communications Commission. (2004, January 20). *Media ownership policy reexamination.* Retrieved January 19, 2006, from the FCC Web site: http://www.fcc.gov/ownership/.

7. Ahrens, F. (2005, January 28). FCC drops bid to relax media rules. *The Washington Post.* Retrieved January 19, 2006, from http://www.washingtonpost.com/wp-dyn/articles/A42134-2005Jan27.html.

8. McCullagh, D., & Charny, B. (2005, January 21). *Mixed legacy for FCC's Powell.* Retrieved January 19, 2006, from the CNet Web site: http://news.com.com/Mixed+legacy+for+FCCs+Powell/2100-1033_3-5545030.html.

9. Labaton, S. (2005, January 22). Powell to step down at FCC after pushing for deregulation. *The New York Times.* Retrieved January 19, 2006, from http://www.nytimes.com/2005/01/22/politics/22powell.html?ex=1137819600&en=ce9c30b950513a8a&ei=5070.

10. Shales, T. (2004, November 21). Michael Powell exposed! The FCC chairman has no clothes. *The Washington Post.* Retrieved January 19, 2006, from http://www.washingtonpost.com/wp-dyn/articles/A62718-2004Nov19.html.

11. Preciphs, J. (2005, January 26). Digital divide shortchanged, advocates say. *The Washington Times.* Retrieved January 19, 2006, from http://www.washtimes.com/upi-breaking/20050126-121105-3611r.htm.

12. Clyburn, J. E. (2001, February 14). *FCC should not ignore the digital divide.* Retrieved January 19, 2006, from http://www.house.gov/apps/list/speech/sc06_clyburn/cc010214digitaldivide.html.

13. Powell, M. K. (2003, October 23). *Diversity in the legal profession: Opening the pipeline.* Speech presented at the American Bar Association Summit, Washington, DC.

14. Federal Communications Commission. (n.d.). *Biography of Michael Powell.* Retrieved January 19, 2006, from http://www.fcc.gov/commissioners/previous/powell/biography.html.

Chapter 12

Reverend Jesse L. Jackson, Sr.
Founder and President, Rainbow/PUSH Coalition

AP/WIDE WORLD PHOTOS/LYNSEY ADDARIO

PUSHING BEYOND GOVERNMENT POLICIES AND PROGRAMS

When former President Bill Clinton toured the nation in 2000 to draw attention to the need for the government and private agencies to help close the nation's digital divide, he visited East Palo Alto, CA. In a speech before community residents, he said he had been looking at the classified advertising section of the local newspaper and found more than 10,000 positions open in nearby Silicon Valley. "The problem," he said, "is that there aren't enough skilled bodies to go around. If these jobs could be filled by all of the unemployed people here in East Palo Alto, what a different world this would be today."[1]

Earlier in 1999, civil rights activist Jesse L. Jackson, Sr., had already begun working in East Palo Alto to change the employment picture and to bring more African Americans into high-tech jobs and businesses in the capital of the information technology industry. Jackson started the Silicon Valley Project (SVP) as part of his activist organization, the Rainbow/PUSH (People United to Serve Humanity) Coalition.[2] SVP sought to change conditions for African Americans and other minorities by advocating for the inclusion of people of color on the boards of directors and executive staff of the top Silicon Valley high-tech companies, building digital connections between minority-owned businesses and the high tech industry, and opening up access to capital for minority businesses, venture funds, and technology entrepreneurs.

Jackson's project is a nongovernmental, nonprofit agency that extended his civil rights activism to the Information Revolution. He had already been successful with a similar project in the financial district of New York City. The Wall Street Project (WSP) was founded by Jackson in 1997 on the birthday of Dr. Martin Luther King, Jr., to promote inclusion, opportunity, and economic growth by encouraging public and private industries to improve hiring and promotion practices; name more minorities to corporate boards; allocate more business to minority companies; and increase the amount of business that minority firms conduct with each other. Using WSP as a model, SVP runs several programs and initiatives to increase the participation of African Americans and other minorities in the economic prosperity of the digital revolution.

CLOSING THE DIVIDE IN SILICON VALLEY

Working through SVP in East Palo Alto, Jackson partnered with Hewlett Packard (HP) and numerous East Palo Alto agencies on a comprehensive "digital village" initiative.[3] This program brought together a variety of services and technological products to schools, area businesses, and local nonprofit organizations. At the same time, SVP attracted more than 1,000 people to its annual technology conferences to discuss employment challenges, digital diversity, and corporate culture in Silicon Valley, access to capital for women and minorities, and other relevant subjects.

Speaking at the Rainbow/PUSH Digital Connections Conference in 2003, former HP chief executive officer Carly Fiorina pointed out the many things that had been accomplished in East Palo Alto through collaboration between her corporation and Jackson's SVP.[4]

If we have learned anything in this economy, we have learned that opportunity is not just good economic policy, it is good business. Inclusion isn't just good social policy, it is good business. Diversity isn't just good community policy, it is increasingly not only good business, but it is what separates winners from losers in the marketplace.

Fiorina touted the achievements of HP and Jackson's SVP in East Palo Alto. HP put teams of its best and brightest employees in different communities for a period of up to three years to work with local citizens to set goals and create solutions for the challenges that the community faced. They called these communities digital villages, and the first was East Palo Alto. Working with SVP and HP, the people of East Palo Alto created a small business development initiative. They have worked with more than 100 businesses, created more than 150 jobs, and generated almost $3 million in revenue in the past two years, according to Fiorina. The effort was also targeted toward schools. Schools in the local community received new laptops on which students, parents, and teachers were trained. The use of information technology helped to increase students' average grade point average and reading level.

The people of East Palo Alto also created an online resource center that provided the city's residents and organizations with information about the community and the city. To help people access this information, they created welcoming technology access points, where local residents learned how to use computers and access the Internet.

Using the lessons learned from Palo Alto, Jackson and Fiorina also worked to build on the 1,000 Churches Connected Initiative, which Jackson launched in 2001. This effort brings technology access centers to church basements across the country.[5,6] Fiorina said that the experience in Palo Alto had allowed her corporation to build next-generation digital villages in India, South Africa, and other parts of the world. In the meantime, almost 200 businesses have joined with Jackson and established a collaborative council of technology companies and minority businesses to promote and develop more business opportunities in the technology arena.

BEGINNING THE FOURTH STAGE OF THE CIVIL RIGHTS MOVEMENT

Jackson believes that his efforts in Silicon Valley are helping to move African Americans into what he sees as the fourth stage of the civil rights movement.[7,8] Speaking before the Commonwealth Club in Silicon Valley, Jackson said that it was a national disgrace that in 1999 there was only one African American at a top Silicon Valley high-tech company.[9]

In order to ensure full participation in the Information Age, this technological revolution must be accompanied by a revolution in attitude. A revolutionary new understanding of the value of each community—from Wall Street to the Mississippi Delta. A revolutionary new understanding of our role in the free market, our role in ensuring that the market works on perfect information.

Jackson believes that when African Americans "supply companies with large portions of their market and revenues and ... the corporations don't contract with people of color, don't have any people of color above middle management or on their board of directors, they boycott us even though our consumer dollars keeps the company in business." He believes that the next civil rights battle must include making sure that African American-owned businesses get contracts and access to investment capital, training youth to move into technology, and ensuring that tech companies stop "boycotting" Black consumers. Jackson said that his work in getting more involved in prosperity through technology is part of Dr. Martin Luther King's last assignment. That assignment is for African Americans to use their private consumer power to leverage companies for reciprocal trade.

To put his words into action, Jackson attempted to raise about $100,000 to buy stock in Silicon Valley's fifty largest publicly traded companies.[10,11] The stock purchase would be an extension of the strategy that the civil rights leader used on Wall Street: buying stock as leverage to get corporate executives and boards of directors to embrace diversity. Jackson planned to use donations and investments from a network of supporters to buy stock in companies such as Intel Corporation, Microsoft Corporation, HP, Apple Computer, Applied Materials, and Oracle Corporation.

In the Information Revolution, Jackson believes African Americans should be "shareholders, not sharecroppers." In his address to the Commonwealth Club, he said that changing the high-tech industry to include African Americans requires progress on several fronts. First, coalition partnerships must be forged among government, business, civil groups, and other institutions to educate, train, and employ African Americans in the Information Technology industries. Second, Silicon Valley companies should educate, train, recruit, and employ nearly 2,000 workers from America. Jackson believes that technology companies should not rely so much on workers from abroad to fill high-tech positions in Silicon Valley companies. Finally, he believes that African American youths should be challenged to pursue math, science, and business degrees in order to participate fully in the high-tech society of the future.

BIOGRAPHY

Jackson was born in 1941 in Greenville, SC.[12] He graduated from the public schools in Greenville and then enrolled in the University of Illinois on a football scholarship. He later transferred to North Carolina A&T State University and graduated in 1964. He began his theological studies at the Chicago Theological Seminary but deferred his studies when he began working full-time in the civil rights movement. Jackson received his earned Master of Divinity degree in 2000. He began his activism as a student in summer 1960 seeking to desegregate the local public library in Greenville and then as a leader in the sit-in movement. In 1965, he became a full-time orga-nizer for the Southern Christian Leadership Conference (SCLC). He was soon appointed by Dr. Martin Luther King, Jr., to direct SCLC's Operation Breadbasket program. In December 1971, Jackson founded Operation PUSH in Chicago. The goals of Operation PUSH were economic empowerment and expanding educational, business, and employment opportunities for the disadvantaged and people of color. In 1984, Jackson founded the National Rainbow Coalition, a national social justice organization based in Washington, DC, devoted to political empowerment, education, and changing public policy. In September 1996, the Rainbow Coalition and Operation PUSH merged into the Rainbow/PUSH Coalition to continue the work of both approaches and maximize resources.

In 1984 and 1988, Jackson made unsuccessful bids to become president of the United States. During his campaigns, however, his organizations registered millions of new voters. In 1990, in an im-pressive victory, Jackson was elected to the post of U.S. Senator from Washington, DC, a position also known as "statehood senator." The office was created to advocate for statehood for the District of Columbia, which has a greater population than five states but no voting representation in Congress.[13,14]

Jackson has acted many times as an international diplomat in sen-sitive political situations. In 1984, he secured the release of captured Navy Lieutenant Robert Goodman from Syria and the release of 48

Cuban and Cuban American prisoners in Cuba. He was the first American to bring hostages out of Kuwait and Iraq in 1990. In 1999, Jackson negotiated the release of U.S. soldiers held hostage in Kosovo.

Jackson has also been a consistent and vigorous supporter of the labor movement in the United States and worldwide. Jackson is known as someone who has walked more picket lines and spoken at more labor rallies than any other national leader. He has worked with unions to organize workers, to protect workers' rights, and to mediate labor disputes. In 1996, he traveled to Asia to investigate the treatment of workers in the Japanese automobile industry and in athletic apparel factories in Indonesia.

Jackson has received numerous honors for his work in human and civil rights and his promotion of nonviolent social change. He has been on the Gallup List of the Ten Most Respected Americans for more than a dozen years. He has received the prestigious National Association for the Advancement of Colored People's Spingarn Award in addition to honors from hundreds of grassroots, civic, and community organizations from coast to coast. Jackson has received more than 40 honorary doctorate degrees and frequently lectures at major colleges and universities, including Howard, Yale, Princeton, Morehouse, Harvard, Columbia, Stanford, and Hampton. The most prestigious honor yet came on August 9, 2000, when President Bill Clinton awarded Jackson the Presidential Medal of Freedom, the nation's highest civilian honor. The presidential medal typifies a life of service and a concern for the least fortunate.

From 1992 to 2000, Jackson hosted "Both Sides With Jackson" on Cable News Network. He continues to write a weekly column of analysis, which is syndicated by the *Chicago Tribune/Los Angeles Times*. He is the author of two books: *Keep Hope Alive* and *Straight From the Heart*. In 1996, Jackson coauthored *Legal Lynching: Racism, Injustice, and the Death Penalty* and *It's About the Money* with his son, U.S. Representative Jesse L. Jackson, Jr.

In October 1997, President Bill Clinton and Secretary of State Madeleine Albright appointed Jackson as special envoy of the president and secretary of state for the promotion of democracy in Africa. In this official position, Jackson traveled to several countries on the African continent and met with such national leaders as President Nelson Mandela of the Republic of South Africa, His Excellency Daniel T. Arap Moi of Kenya, and President Frederick J. T. Chiluba of Zambia. In 2003, he traveled to several African counties on an unofficial basis to help stimulate trade and to aid the continent in participating in the global information revolution.[15]

Jackson married Jacqueline Lavinia Brown in 1963. They have five children: Santita Jackson, Congressman Jesse L. Jackson, Jr., Jonathan Luther Jackson, Yusef DuBois Jackson, Esq, and Jacqueline Lavinia Jackson, Jr.

NOTES

1. Lilleston, R. (2000, April 17). *Clinton highlights public-private partnership to bridge technology gap.* Retrieved January 17, 2006, from the CNN Web site: http://archives.cnn.com/2000/ALLPOLITICS/stories/04/17/digital.divide/.

2. Evangelista, B. (1999, February 3). Jackson joins digital divide job groups. *San Francisco Chronicle.* Retrieved January 14, 2006, from http://www.sfgate.com/cgi-bin/article.cgi?file=/chronicle/archive/1999/02/03/BU81977.DTL&type=printable.

3. Bowman, L. M. (2003, May 1). *Fiorina urges companies to combat the digital divide.* Retrieved January 14, 2006, from ZD NET UK Web site: http://news.zdnet.co.uk/business/0,39020645,2134154,00.htm.

4. Fiorina, C. (2003, April 30). *Remarks.* Speech presented at the Rainbow/ Push Digital Connections Conference, San Jose, CA.

5. Rainbow/PUSH Silicon Valley Project. (n.d.). *How we build e-connections.* Retrieved January 17, 2006, from http://www.siliconvalleyproject.net/ Programs.html.

6. Rainbow/PUSH Coalition. (2006, January 10). *Rainbow PUSH Wall Street Project announces plan to connect African-American churches, achieve collective economic prosperity.* Retrieved January 18, 2006, from http://www.rainbowpush.org/rpc.

7. Jackson, J. L., Sr. (n.d.). *My last assignment.* Retrieved January 17, 2006, from The Black Collegian Online Web site: http://www.black-collegian.com/african/assignment402.shtml.

8. Jackson, J. L., Sr. (1999, July 14). *Rebuilding the house: The fourth movement of the freedom symphony.* Speech presented at the 90th Annual Convention of the National Association for the Advancement of Colored People, New York, NY.

9. Jackson, J. L., Sr. (1999, October 5). *From digital divide to digital opportunity.* Speech presented to The Commonwealth Club, San Francisco, CA.

10. Evangelista, B. (1999, March 2). Preaching inclusion: Jesse Jackson takes stock of diversity in Silicon Valley. *San Francisco Chronicle.* Retrieved January 14, 2006, from http://programmersguild.org/archives/lib/race/sfc19990302diversity.htm.

11. Jackson, J. L., Sr. (1999, September 14). *Disconnected not connected, excluded not included.* Speech presented to the National Association of Minorities in Cable, New York.

12. Rainbow/PUSH Coalition. (n.d.). *The Reverend Jesse Louis Jackson, Sr.* Retrieved January 17, 2006, from http://www.rainbowpush.org/rpc.

13. The Good Shepherd Restoration Ministries, Inc. (2001). *Rev. Jesse L. Jackson, Sr.* Retrieved January 17, 2006, from http://www.tgsrm.org/Jackson.html.

14. Timmerman, K. R. (2001). *Shakedown exposing the Real Jesse Jackson.* Washington, DC: Regnery Publishing.

15. Rainbow/PUSH Coalition. (2000, February 9). *Jackson trade mission bridges digital divide.* Retrieved January 18, 2006, from http://www.rainbowpush.org/rpc.

PART III
Educators and Professionals

A key aspect of the universal access component of the 1996 telecommunications law was that all Americans must be able to access the national and global information infrastructures for the purpose of education. Like never before, the world of work is looking for people who are empowered by communicative skills, analytical abilities, foresight, and capacities to formulate strategic policies. Employers want workers who have had access to sophisticated information and communications technologies. The way young people are educated has a direct bearing on their ability to become the information workers of the future. Throughout America, many African Americans are leading the effort to educate a new generation of people using technology or are actively trying to get more young people involved in information technology careers. Several of them are profiled in Part III.

Dr. John B. Slaughter runs a national organization that raises money to educate African Americans and other minorities to become computer engineering professionals. Dr. Slaughter is a renowned engineer who helped to computerize the U.S. Navy's weapons systems during his distinguished career.

In California, Dean LeBaron Woodyard's vision and hard work have helped to bring distance learning and educational technology to the California community colleges, the largest system of higher education in the world. The system gives citizens access to an education whether or not they can attend traditional classroom settings.

In Florida, Dr. Dhyana Ziegler is using virtual reality and other technologies to train young people in mathematics and science. She has been instrumental in the development of Florida's virtual school system, which is a model for the rest of the nation.

Chapter 13

Dr. John B. Slaughter

President and Chief Executive Officer, National Action Council for Minorities in Engineering

EDUCATING THE FUTURE LEADERS OF THE INFORMATION REVOLUTION

"There is no greater challenge today than the inclusion of all our citizens in the benefits of the twenty-first century technological revolution."[1] Speaking of the need to include more African Americans and other minorities in information technology (IT) careers, Dr. Shirley A. Jackson, president of Rensselaer Polytechnic Institute, said these words at the 2000 Annual Conference of the National Action Council for Minorities in Engineering (NACME). In the same address, she praised and congratulated John B. Slaughter for becoming president and chief executive officer of NACME at a time when the organization is providing more computer engineering scholarship support to African Americans and other minorities than any other private organization in the nation. Slaughter was named to this position in June 2000 after a prominent, distinguished, and multifaceted career as engineer, scientist, government executive, and college president. His work at NACME, however, is having a significant impact on the development of future African American leaders of the Information Revolution.

IT is continuing to expand and be an important part of our lives. For African Americans not to be involved in that process would place us further behind. I'm encouraging young people to get involved and take the right courses. You have to be prepared.[2]

In 2004–2005, about 30 percent of NACME scholars went into IT fields such as computer engineering, computer science, and information systems.[3] During the same time, nearly half of the NACME scholars were from African American backgrounds, and many of them went into IT disciplines. In this 1-year period, NACME provided approximately 250 scholarships to African American students to pursue careers in IT.

Increasing the number of African Americans in the field of IT is still a daunting task in light of the many challenges that face this group and the challenges of becoming computer engineers and IT specialists. Slaughter believes that one of the greatest problems is that African American high school graduates too often do not take the prerequisite mathematics and science courses to even consider engineering study.

NACME was created in 1974 to help increase workplace diversity in engineering by providing support to African Americans, other minorities, and women in technology fields. To help African Americans and other minorities prepare for careers in technology, under Slaughter's leadership NACME has developed a program called "Math Is Power."

It's helping parents and young people understand the importance of studying mathematics in elementary, middle and high schools, and why you have to have mathematics if you're going to study engineering at a university. What we've learned is those students who've been exposed to the campaign are much more knowledgeable about the importance of mathematics than those who haven't.[4]

Math Is Power tries to reach young people and their parents, but according to Slaughter many African Americans have not taken advantage of it because they still do not have computer access. Slaughter has put in place other programs such as Guide Me NACME and M2W (MidSchool to Workplace) to help African Americans and other minorities to prepare for careers in computer engineering.

Slaughter is motivated by the fact that more engineers are needed in America than ever before. Under his guidance, NACME has expanded its reach into high schools by establishing the Engineering Vanguard Program.[5] This program nurtures at-risk students and provides them with training programs and support. From these activities, NACME is learning what ingredients are needed to make it possible for students to be successful in studying engineering.

Slaughter was at the helm when NACME celebrated its 30th anniversary in 2004. He launched a block grant scholarship program, restructured its fundraising arm, initiated a strategic planning for the future, and removed the financial deficits that had plagued the organization for the previous 2½ years.[6] Now Slaughter is focusing his attention on the significantly lower retention rate of underrepresented minority engineering students compared with that of their White and Asian peers. Approximately 40 percent of entering minority students nationwide graduate compared with 70 percent for White and Asian students. According to Slaughter, the reasons for the difference in graduation rates are many and include the relatively poor academic preparation of many minority students and the lack of adequate financial resources available to complete their studies.

EXCELLENCE AND EQUITY

Slaughter believes that in order for African Americans to be successful in technology in the future, they must gain access to the educational opportunities available in the nation's most selective universities. Slaughter wants to graduate 250,000 minority engineering students over the next decade,[7] doubling the output of the last 30 years. At the current rate, about 10 percent of those graduates would be African American. According to Slaughter, more graduates would translate to an increase in the number of African Americans who receive PhDs in engineering and thus become qualified to teach in the nation's universities:

Although I am encouraged by the number of students in engineering from historically underrepresented minorities, I remain discouraged by the small number of minority faculty members in science and engineering. The argument often advanced by colleges and universities that there aren't enough minority PhDs in science and engineering in the pipeline is not as tenable as it was a few years ago.

According to Slaughter, about 1 percent of engineering faculties nationwide are African American or Latino, a situation that has not improved in the past 20 years, even though the number of Black and Brown PhDs in science and engineering increases every year and more and more of them are available and fully prepared for faculty appointments.[8] Slaughter believes that America requires all of the scientific and engineering talent it can muster to maintain a competitive edge in the global marketplace: "Failure to address the inequalities that exist in our educational systems, especially in higher education, could doom us to a position of technological inferiority among the principal nations of the world."

DIGITIZING THE U.S. NAVY

Ironically, there was no organization like NACME in existence to help Slaughter when he was a young man. Nevertheless, he made a significant contribution to America, becoming a world leader in technology early in his career as a computer engineer. From 1960 to 1975, Slaughter was the physical science administrator for information systems at the Naval Electronics Laboratory Center (NELC) at Point Loma, CA. In this position, he worked on technological innovations that changed the U.S. Navy's capability to be a dominant military force on the oceans of the world.

"I led a team that tested the first navy digital computer for use in warfare," he said.[9] "Back in 1965, we did the first experiments in using a digital computer as the control system for large weapons systems. We did the first demonstration of using a computer for a closed-loop control system."

Before this, the U.S. Navy did not even use digital computers to run weapons systems on warships, relying instead on expensive, complex, and sometimes unreliable analog computers. Attacks on ships in the early 1950s by high-speed enemy jet fighters necessitated more compact computers that could rapidly assist battle managers in conducting antiair defense. Under Slaughter's leadership, a team at NELC was charged with assembling the hardware, performing tests, and developing such a computer system.[10] Slaughter devised a digital computer system that controlled the position of guns with digital sampled data control algorithms, and he implemented a radar-directed digital gunfire control solution. The digital computer and its program also computed corrections to stabilize the radar and gun mount for the rolling motions of a ship at sea. In 1963,

Slaughter completed these designs at the NELC and in 1965 demonstrated that his computer programs could run a digital computer to control a massive weapons system on a ship. He also worked out solutions for using digital computer-controlled systems for rocket launchers, radar systems, and steam propulsion mechanisms. Slaughter's work was instrumental in enabling the U.S. Navy to convert its entire fleet from analog to digital control of shipboard systems. For most people, helping to shape the direction of naval warfare for the future would be an achievement of a lifetime. For Slaughter, however, it was just the beginning of long list of personal achievements in the fields of engineering, science, and education.

FROM ENGINEER TO ACADEMIC ADMINISTRATOR

After his 15-year stint at NELC, in 1975, Slaughter was tapped as director of the Applied Physics Laboratory of the University of Washington. In 1977, he was appointed assistant director for astronomics, atmospherics, and earth and ocean sciences at the National Science Foundation (NSF) in Washington, DC. Also in 1977 he served as editor of the *International Journal of Computers and Electrical Engineering*. From 1979 to 1980, he was provost and academic vice president at Washington State University.

In the 1980s, Slaughter became a national leader in the scientific community when former President Jimmy Carter named him to head the nation's top scientific organization.[11] From 1980 to 1982, he was the first African American director of the NSF, the chief federal government agency for support of scientific research and improvements in science education. At that time, the agency had an annual budget of $1 billion.

In 1982, Slaughter was elected to membership in the National Academy of Engineering. During the same year, he became the first African American chancellor of the University of Maryland, College Park.[12] This campus was predominantly White, with about 38,000 students and 2,000 teachers and an annual budget of $458 million. He served in this position from 1982 to 1988 and attempted to make major advances in recruitment and retention of African American students and faculty. As it turned out, however, his greatest challenge was the university's sports program.[13] During his tenure, star basketball player and Boston Celtics draft pick Len Bias died in a drug scandal that rocked the university. Slaughter overcame the turmoil that ensued and moved on to another achievement in higher education.

In 1988, the trustees of Occidental College in Los Angeles selected Slaughter from a field of 150 educators to be their president. Once again, he was the first African American to serve in the position, and he became a member of an elite group of Blacks who have been presidents at predominantly White institutions of higher learning. He served at Occidental College from 1988 through July 1999, when he was named president emeritus.[14,15] During this time, Slaughter promoted the idea that "college education is the road to success and that access can be given without compromising standards." He anticipated the changes that were emerging in southern California and guided the university toward more multiculturalism.[16] Since then, he has expounded on the notion that engineering schools can give access to African Americans and other minorities without compromising education standards.

BIOGRAPHY

Slaughter was born on March 16, 1934. The only son of four children of a janitor and a homemaker, he grew up in Topeka, KS, in the days before Brown vs. Board of Education opened up new opportunities for minority students in the city's primary schools.

Even though I was very much interested in engineering and would tell anyone who would listen that I planned to attend either the University of Kansas or Kansas State to study engineering, I ended up being shunted off into a vocational track. Back then—and unfortunately it still happens too often now—teachers and counselors simply didn't envision minority kids wanting to pursue the path that I did. There just wasn't much encouragement for any of us to consider a scientific career. In fact, you'd get discouraged. You really had to want to do it.

Slaughter not only wanted to do it but taught himself early in life by doing projects from *Popular Mechanics* and *Popular Science* magazines. He made cameras and repaired radios for fun. He and his father eventually turned his ingenuity into a backyard business. The money that they earned from Slaughter's revamping radios and other electronic devices was used to purchase test equipment and build a radio shop in their own backyard. The encouragement of his parents and these early experiences served as the foundation for his later achievements in life.

After high school, Slaughter went to Kansas State University (KSU), putting himself through school by working as a lab assistant and a janitor. Slaughter was the only African American in his engineering class.

He received a Bachelor of Science degree in electrical engineering from KSU in 1956, was awarded a Master of Science in engineering from the University of California, Los Angeles in 1961, and received his PhD in engineering sciences from the University of California, San Diego in 1971. John Slaughter served as an Electronics Engineer for General Dynamics from 1956 to 1960. Slaughter sometimes jokes that he is the first Black engineer whom he ever met. In 1987, however, he was honored with the first U.S. Black Engineer of the Year award and was named to the American Society for Engineering Education Hall of Fame in 1993. Now Slaughter is a leader in the education, engineering, and scientific communities. He has served on the Committee on Minorities in Engineering and chairs the Action Forum on Engineering Workforce Diversity for the National Academy of Engineering. Slaughter is a fellow of the American Association for the Advancement of Science, Institute of Electrical and Electronic Engineers, and American Academy of Arts and Sciences.

Slaughter holds honorary degrees from more than twenty institutions. He won the Martin Luther King, Jr., National Award in 1997 and UCLA's Medal of Excellence in 1989. He is the founding editor of the international journal *Computers & Electrical Engineering* and serves as a director of Solutia, Inc. and IBM.

Slaughter and his wife of 45 years, Dr. Bernice Slaughter, have two children, Dr. John Brooks Slaughter, Jr., and Mrs. Jacqueline Michelle Slaughter-Bolden.

NOTES

1. Jackson, S. A. (2000, October 26). *Continental divide: The digital divide and the technology pipeline.* Forum presented at the Annual Conference of the National Action Council for Minorities in Engineering, Long Beach, CA.

2. John B. Slaughter, personal communication, March 15, 2005.

3. National Action Council for Minorities in Engineering. (n.d.). *Annual Report 2004.* Retrieved June 14, 2005, from http://www.nacme.org/04/.

4. John B. Slaughter, personal communication, March 15, 2005.

5. Podolsky, E. *Staying on track.* Retrieved June 9, 2005, from the Graduating Engineer & Computer Careers Online Web site: http://www.graduatingengineer.com/ articles/feature/10-30-01e.html.

6. Slaughter, J. B. (2005). *Speeches and reflections from NACME's leader: 2004: Year-end report.* Retrieved June 28, 2005, from NACME Web site: http://www.nacme.org/news/prescorner.html.

7. Slaughter, J. B. (2003, April 10). *The search for excellence and equity in higher education: A perspective from an engineer.* The George W. Woodruff

School of Mechanical Engineering Annual Distinguished Lecture presented at Georgia Tech University, Atlanta.

8. Slaughter, J. B. (2005). *Speeches and reflections from NACME's leader: 2004 Bueche Award presented to John Brooks Slaughter.* Retrieved June 28, 2005, from NACME Web site: http://www.nacme.org/news/prescorner. html.

9. John B. Slaughter, personal communication, March 15, 2005.

10. Boslaugh, D. L. (1999). *When computers went to sea: The digitization of the United States Navy.* Los Alamitos, CA: IEEE Computer Society and the Society of Naval Architects and Engineers.

11. Associated Press. (1980, July 4). Carter names new head of U.S. Science Agency. *The Washington Post.* Retrieved June 11, 2005, from http:// proquest.umi.com/pdf/8da2f54e0056c31ca1cdeaee1492e6d3/1118505489/ share2/pqimage/hnirs2/20050611112809208/6396/out.pdf.

12. Feinberg, L. (1982, June 6). Chancellor named for Maryland; Engineer will head College Park Campus; Science Agency Chief to head U-MD campus. *The Washington Post.* Retrieved June 11, 2005, from http:// proquest.umi.com/pdf/8da2f54e0056c31ca1cdeaee1492e6d3/1118505489/ share2/pqimage/hnirs2/20050611112809208/6396/out.pdf.

13. Fenton, J. (2005, February 24). *Weathering the storm.* Retrieved June 9, 2005, from the *Diamondback* Online Web site: http://www.diamondbackonline. com/vnews/display.v/ART/2005/02/24/421d6eee26596.

14. Schrader, E. (1988, April 2). Educators hail the hiring of Black as head of Occidental. *The Los Angeles Times.* Retrieved June 11, 2005, from http://pqasb.pqarchiver.com/latimes/59776135.html?MAC=3c168aa75e409 3eae4e11acfcf4e1e6e&did=59776135&FMT=FT&FMTS=FT&date=Apr+2%2C +1988&author=ESTHER+SCHRADER&printformat=&desc=Educators+Hail+ the+Hiring+of+Black+as+Head+of+Occidental.

15. Gordon, L. (1988, September 6). His success is all academic: The former president of the University of Maryland is settling in at Occidental College with the expectation of "breaking new ground." *The Los Angeles Times.* Retrieved June 11, 2005, from http://pqasb.pqarchiver.com/latimes/ 59876039.html?MAC=7392699358aaab12cbeecea8bed9b85f&did=5987603 9&FMT=FT&FMTS=FT&date=Sep+6%2C+1988&author=LARRY+GORDON& printformat=&desc=His+Success+Is+All+Academic+The+former+president+ of+the+University+of+Maryland+is+settling+in+at+Occidental+College+with+ the+expectation+of+%60breaking+new+ground.%27.

16. Mithers, C. L. (1999, May). Welcome to Multicultural U. *Los Angeles Times Magazine,* pp. 11–13.

Chapter 14

LeBaron Woodyard
Dean of Academic Affairs and Instructional Resources, California Community Colleges

BUILDING A NETWORK FOR HIGHER EDUCATION

When Arnold Schwarzenegger delivered his first commencement address as governor of the state of California, it was to the 2005 Santa Monica College graduating class.[1] Governor Schwarzenegger chose to speak at this community college because it is his alma mater.

"California's community colleges are critical to maintaining and improving our first class higher education system and preparing our students to meet the demands of our economy," Governor Schwarzenegger said during the ceremony. He pledged that, as governor and a former community college student, he was committed to ensuring that California community colleges provide affordable, quality education to the state's students.

LeBaron Woodyard's vision and hard work have helped to make Governor Schwarzenegger's goal more attainable. The California community colleges (CCC) make up the largest system of higher education in the world. The system connects 109 colleges

and 72 districts, which provide educational, vocational, and transfer programs to more than 2.6 million students each academic
year.[2] From 1994 to 2002, Woodyard envisioned, developed, and
implemented an educational technology network for the CCC.
Called 4CNet, the network was a telecommunications and technology system that provided a backbone for online and distance education for students throughout the entire CCC system. Woodyard
is currently the dean of Academic Affairs and Instructional
Resources for the Chancellor's Office and is responsible for administering programs that impact the curriculum and instructional
activities of all CCC teachers and students. Before this, Woodyard
was the dean of Technology and Communications. It was in this
position that he planned and implemented a system of education
that used computers, Internet, satellite, and cable television to
make up a network providing educational opportunities to Californians even when they could not attend campus classroom
sessions.

This was not the first system of its type in the country but it was the largest
and everyone was taking a look at it. One in ten higher education students
in America is a CCC student. The CCC population represents 10 percent of
the college student population in the country. Within community colleges,
the CCC population represents 25 percent of the community college student
population in the country.[3]

The 4CNet initiative grew out of a need to service a growing population of students in the CCC system by allowing educators to use
new technology. In the early 1990s, Woodyard's job at the CCC was
to develop programs that helped instructors to improve their teaching. While reviewing teachers' proposals for improvements, he
noticed that teachers wanted more educational technology in the
classroom. Working in the Chancellor's Office, Woodyard incorporated the needs of the instructors into budget change proposals that
went to the state of California's legislative review process. It was
through this process that he received funding for new educational
technology and 4CNet. The statewide CCC telecommunications and
technology system was funded in the 1996 State Budget Act
and called the Technology and Telecommunications Infrastructure
Program.

Woodyard also solicited funding from external sources. He was
awarded grants from the U.S. Department of Commerce to develop a
telecommunications plan for the CCC system. In 1994, he wrote a

telecommunication grant proposal to plan a system that would include Internet, satellite, telephones, telecommunications infrastructure lines, and video conferencing: CCC's Technology I Strategic Plan (Tech I). This strategic study identified the need for a statewide telecommunications and technology system to effectively carry out the mission of the CCC. He submitted his plan to the state and was awarded $9.3 million to implement it. This included revamping and automating all libraries in the system. The first year of operation was 1996–1997.

In a 1997 message to the CCC community, Woodyard said, "The establishment of 4CNet allows the CCC system to develop and sustain a competitive edge in providing training for California business and industry, meet the needs of today's adult learner, and have a positive impact on the physical environment of the state in the areas of air quality, fuel consumption, and transportation systems."[4]

In 1998, the 4CNet entered its first full year of deployment, and the network and connections to it were operationalized over a 2-year period. The network continued to expand to meet the needs of the growing CCC system. Building on the 4CNet, the CCC later created the California Virtual University (CVU) and the California Virtual Campus (CVC) as gateways to technology-mediated distance learning courses and programs. The CVU was funded in 1998–1999 for $2.9 million to provide a 24-hours-a-day, 7-days-a-week learning environment for students.

Advancing to the next level, Woodyard led the team that developed Technology II Strategic Plan (Tech II), the second plan for the period 2000–2005.[5–8] The goal was a systemwide technology plan that would build on Tech I, encourage expanded use of technology, and continue to support the mission of the CCC. Tech II has fostered long-range strategic plans at colleges for using technology in teaching and learning, increasing student access, improving student support services, and achieving increased efficiency and effectiveness in administrative support. The funding and activities of the CVU/CVC program were included as part of the overall goals of Tech II. Tech II involved creating an infrastructure to support the system across all campuses. This required a $93 million budget.

Woodyard's proposal was initially denied, but Woodyard endured and the program eventually reached the $122 million level. Tech II's primary goal was to aid California students in having "access and success" in their pursuit of educational goals. It was an ambitious plan that included access to computers for students, faculty, and staff; training for the faculty in the use of the information technology tools; expansion of multimedia classrooms and student computer labs; and improving faculty and student access to automated library and learning resources. The plan also included the establishment of a new leadership role in the CCC Chancellor's Office to spearhead the new body of work and expectations defined by Tech II. The new proposal includes a complete system upgrade. A satellite television system, for example, generates eight channels of video for learning, and the Cooperational Networks in California (CNIC) connects the entire education system from kindergarten through college. However, Woodyard's original network is still at their core.

When the 4CNet was being transferred to the new system, the president of CNIC said, "Currently, the circuits serving the CSU campuses, the community colleges and K-12 schools are transitioning from the 4CNet backbone to the new CalREN backbone.[9] While we hail the coming of the new infrastructure, we say farewell to 4CNet, which has served CSU for 2 decades, the community colleges for nearly a decade, and the K-12 for the past 3 years. 4CNet was a pioneer in educational networking. It laid the foundation for CENIC to be able to bring the entire education and research community to our new multi-tiered CalREN environment."

AFRICAN AMERICANS AND THE FUTURE

Woodyard believes that distance education and online learning is a benefit to Black students and that the CCC system helps to reduce the digital divide. He oversees the Math, Engineering and Science Administration, which provides online courses in math.

"If Blacks are going to get into [information technology] they will have to go through math," he said.[10] "Algebra is one of the gatekeeper courses provided in the MESA program." Studies conducted by the Board of Governors of the CCC have shown that Blacks participate in distance education at a higher rate than they do in on-campus programs.

"The system is all-inclusive and from an access point this is the entry point," he added. "We try to create a viable system that is technologically robust. We extend the reach even further. The satellite cable system allows people to get education services even if they do not have a computer. Courses taken through cable TV can be transferred to the regular system."

The CCC does not have an admissions test. A student simply has to be 18 years old and able to participate in classes. African Americans in California who have some college but have not completed a bachelor's degree can get a fresh start at CCC. Using technology such as CVC and CVU, the CCC aim is to have African Americans and other Californians use the system to help them finish their community college degrees and transfer to institutions of higher learning, such as California State University (CSU). This will increase transfer rates and ultimately the number of African Americans holding degrees. According to Woodyard,

There is a debate. Does technology make teaching and learning better? Does it cause increased learning? I think it does. Intuitively, if you put a student in front of a computer and allow that student to access CCC's Knowledge Net, that is conducive to them without the pressure of seat time. Community labs at libraries and community centers have applications that can help make a difference. CCC is having an impact on Black students through these types of efforts.[11]

BIOGRAPHY

Woodyard was born in Mobile, AL, and is a graduate of CSU. He was an administrator of the Chancellor's Office in the CCC for 15 years. He spent 8 to 10 years developing the systemwide telecommunications plan of the state's community college system. Woodyard's program was moved to the newly created CCC Technology Systems Division.

Woodyard is currently involved with distance education and is developing online instruction. He provides leadership for faculty in developing educational technology tools. As the current dean of Academic Affairs and Educational Services, he is responsible for administering a wide range of programs that impact the curriculum and instructional activities of the system. The challenges of a diverse and large student population and the complex mission of the CCC system are addressed through the work of this administrative unit.

Woodyard plans to be the president of a university one day, and his deanship keeps him on the administrative track. He serves on the Steering Committee for the Western Cooperative for Educational Technology and the Management Development Commission of the Association of California Community College Administrators. He is a much-requested speaker in the area of telecommunications and educational technology and has presented at more than fifty conferences in this area.

NOTES

1. Governor's Office. (2005, June 14). *Governor Schwarzenegger delivers first commencement address at Santa Monica College.* Retrieved August 4, 2005, from http://www.governor.ca.gov/state/govsite/gov_htmldisplay. jsp?sFilePath=/govsite/spotlight/061405_update.htm&sCatTitle=Governor's% 20Update.

2. Board of Governors California Community Colleges. (1999, July 13). *The role of the Chancellor's Office in statewide distance education policy planning for the California Community Colleges.* Retrieved July 11, 2005, from http:// www.cccco.edu/divisions/esed/aa_ir/disted/attachments/08-2sdep.pdf.

3. LeBaron Woodyard, personal communication, November 19, 2004.

4. Woodyard, L. (1997, November). *A message from the Chancellor's Office (part one).* Retrieved July 9, 2005, from the TIPS Online Web site: http://www.tipsnews.org/newsletter/97-11/message1.html.

5. Board of Governors, California Community Colleges. (2000, September). *California community colleges technology II strategic plan.* Retrieved July 11, 2005, from http://www.cccco.edu/divisions/tris/telecom/TechII.html.

6. Chancellor's Office, California Community Colleges. (2001, August). *Distance education report fiscal years 1995–2000.* Retrieved July 11, 2005, from http://www.cccco.edu/divisions/esed/aa_ir/disted/attachments/9-21-01DEReport.doc.

7. Academic Senate for California Community Colleges. (2003, spring). *The impact of computer technology on student access and success in the California community colleges.* Retrieved July 12, 2005, from http:// www.academicsenate.cc.ca.us/Publications/Papers/DigitalDivide.htm.

8. Chancellor's Office, California Community Colleges. (2004, July). *The California virtual campus review report.* Retrieved July 9, 2005, from http:// 64.233.179.104/search?q=cache:922Bjh1qfMUJ:www.siskiyous.edu/staff/crows/ index_files/CVCfinalreport04.doc+LeBaron+Woodyard+%22Virtual%22&hl=en.

9. West, T. (2003, October 31). *The new CalREN network is up and operational.* Retrieved July 11, 2005, from the CENIC Web site: http://www. cenic.org/pubs/c_today/v6_8.htm.

10. LeBaron Woodyard, personal communication, November 19, 2004.

11. LeBaron Woodyard, personal communication, November 19, 2004.

Chapter 15

Dr. Dhyana Ziegler

Assistant Vice President of Instructional Technology and Academic Affairs, Florida Agricultural and Mechanical University

HELPING YOUNG PEOPLE BE CREATIVE IN A VIRTUAL WORLD

Dhyana Ziegler uses virtual reality and other computer technologies to educate African American youth about science and technology and to change the way they perceive career options in information technology (IT) and other science- and computer-related occupations. In Florida, she works through several groundbreaking programs that support her belief that "if we let the children be creative then they will be the Bill Gates of the future." Over the past decade, the state of Florida, National Science Foundation (NSF), American Association for the Advancement of Science (AAAS), and Delta Sigma Theta Sorority, Inc. (DSTS), have supported Ziegler's efforts. She has held several vice presidential-level positions at Florida Agricultural and Mechanical University (FAMU), a historically Black university in Tallahassee. Her innovations in education at the elementary through college levels are helping to spawn a whole new generation of technically literate African Americans.

In October 2000, Florida Governor Jeb Bush appointed Ziegler to the board of trustees of the Florida Virtual Schools (FLVS) and reappointed her for a second term from 2004 to 2006.[1] FLVS is a fully Internet-based public school offering online middle- and high-school curriculum plus a general education diploma (GED) and other test preparation courses. Begun in 1997 with funding from the Florida legislature, FLVS is a 21st-century leader in online education.

Ziegler's appointment to the board of trustees is part of an alliance between FLVS and FAMU through which FAMU prepares its students to go into Florida schools and teach using computers.[2] At the kickoff of this program, Ziegler stated that it would serve as a model for the nation. She believes that all teachers should integrate the use of technology into their teaching.

In 2003, FLVS made available at no cost to Florida teachers and students all the resources and learning materials contained in its Web-based 10th-grade Florida Comprehensive Assessment Test (FCAT) preparation course. The FCAT is part of Florida's overall plan to increase student achievement by implementing higher standards in mathematics, reading, science, and writing. Seventy-two teacher candidates from FAMU used these materials to teach during their required internships in classrooms.

ELIMINATING THE DIGITAL DIVIDE IN FLORIDA

Ziegler has also been remedying disparities in computer access between the haves and the have-nots in communities throughout Florida. She serves as a subject matter expert for the governor's Digital Divide Council,[3,4] created by Bush and the Florida legislature in July 2001 to create reasonable opportunities for all Floridians to access training in skills required to use IT to enhance their quality of life. Through a program called PowerUP, Ziegler has been instrumental in getting computers into communities that would not have them otherwise. PowerUP Florida consists of 23 state-funded programs and 42 programs funded through public and private partnerships.

In 2003, FAMU and the Volunteer Florida Foundation pledged assistance to community groups to hire personnel for educational instruction, purchase nonsoftware curriculum materials, recruit mentors or volunteers, and provide technical support for the computer labs. In the labs, young people in Grades 3 through 8 are learning Web design and various Microsoft programs. Ziegler said that she has been amazed at what young people can do at the PowerUP centers and is looking forward to helping them create software.

On the college level, Ziegler has spearheaded FAMU-UP.[5] She is codirector and the chair of faculty development for the program. Under her direction, a $3.5 million NSF grant has been used to establish a 5-year program that strives toward greater development of education and technology. FAMU-UP uses virtual reality tutorials to teach chemistry and other science to students at the university.

African American students are not excelling in math and science. We created a way for students to better understand by using virtual reality. We shot scientific experiments on video and got animation students to animate them. I have also been working with engineers to look at the Game Boy hardware to see how it can be used for education. Virtual reality should be used to teach science. One of the reasons people don't learn science is that they don't get enough time to participate in it. If people can participate in virtual reality they can learn more.[6]

Ziegler believes that FAMU-UP and other research development programs will produce products that ensure African American students and other people of color have the opportunity to be successful in science, technology, engineering, and mathematics. She believes that this is essential to African Americans becoming major players in the new economy.

Training young people to play a larger role in the computer- and information-based economy of the future is a fundamental goal in Ziegler's work. In addition to her efforts with the state of Florida, she is also a member of the Delta Research and Educational Foundation (DREF), serving as cochair of the Research and Resource Committee.[7,8] The DSTS and DREF, in partnership with the AAAS Directorate for Education and Human Resources Programs, developed and implemented a 5-year Science and Everyday Experiences (SEE) initiative, an informal NSF-funded science education project. The SEE initiative helps parents and caregivers of African American children in kindergarten through Grade 8 develop effective ways to support informal science and mathematics learning experiences. Other partners in this community-based science effort include Radio One, Inc., a conglomerate of 51 radio stations in urban and African

American markets, and The Afro-American Newspaper Company of Baltimore and its affiliated newspapers (circulation of 6.5 million).

PREPARING AFRICAN AMERICANS FOR THE INFORMATION AGE

In 2003, Ziegler used radio to reach out to communities nationwide to better prepare African American parents for their children's careers in computers and other technological occupations.[9,10] Under her direction, DSTS teamed up with a Washington-based talk radio station to bring science and technology information into African American homes. The Delta SEE Connection radio show, hosted by Ziegler, became part of the sorority's ongoing efforts to get young African Americans and their families involved in today's highly technological society. The program was funded by the NSF and produced by DSTS in partnership with WOL Radio, which is owned by Radio One, DREF, and AAAS. The radio series featured African American role models in the science, engineering, and mathematical professions and highlighted scientific research being conducted at private institutions and college campuses, particularly historically Black colleges and universities (HBCUs). (The programs are still available online at www.Deltasee.org.) Ziegler stresses the importance of parents' involvement in shaping their children's success in the technological age.

Ziegler has many concerns about African Americans and the Information Age of the future. She feels that Blacks are not addressing IT and are not positioning themselves to become players in the new information economy, likening it to the old struggle of Blacks not being in control of the broadcast media. Some, she stated, like Richard Parsons are doing well, but most are not.

The Internet was an opportunity because it was colorless. It was an opportunity for Black people to market, produce, and package products. But Blacks did not use this opportunity. Even Blacks' research and culture are not on the Internet. There's no Black Google or Yahoo. Blacks are not in the development part of the Internet. We have not learned how to make money off of this technology. One could say that Blacks are left behind again. This time, however, it's us. We are not stepping up to the plate.[11]

According to Ziegler, HBCUs should play a leading role in preparing young people for the technological future. However, HBCUs are lagging and losing ground because they are not prepared to teach

students what they need to know. She noted that if HBCUs had cor-
roborated on this issue, they could have achieved major success.
Instead, four or five historically White universities (i.e., University of
California, Berkeley) are gaining the monopoly on the future by creating Open Source software. However, she offers encouragement:

The inspiring part is that the door is not closed. I want to teach young Black
people to develop their own software. We need an agenda. We need a plan.
We have to go two generations back to harness software. We need to teach
children in elementary school to create software. We need to have leadership to stand and lead these children and motivate young people through
competition. We need to engage in creative competition with the Cal Techs
and all the others.[12]

Teaching children to work with software as early as possible is an
idea that Ziegler got from her work with the PowerUP program in
Florida. She not only funded training programs but also visited the
sites to observe children's progress. She was impressed with their
capabilities when given the opportunity. Ziegler believes that programs such as PowerUP should be used as incubators to create a
new generation of computer-competent African Americans:

Kid think tanks for kids in elementary to middle school would be the next
step. They should have such programs in school, after school, and home.
The creative think tank would provide 24-hour access. Creative products
would include popular culture art forms coupled with content. Visions
would get encoded in their minds. The future is letting our minds be the
open source. Keeping the mind creative is the open source.[13]

BIOGRAPHY

Ziegler was not reared to be a professorial administrative type with
a grand vision for the technological future. She grew up in New York
City in a music- and entertainment-oriented family.[14] Her father
was a member of a Gospel music group, and as a child, Ziegler
danced and sang. As teenagers, she and her sister won a dance con-
test at the famous Apollo Theater in New York City. Her sister later
married one of the Pips of Gladys Knight and the Pips fame.

Ziegler was always bright and said she was "always doing things
in her head." In fact, she started school as a third-grader at a local
Catholic school. Later she went to the Harlem School of Music,
where she honed her talents, playing guitar and keyboard and
singing and dancing. Ziegler initially planned to go into the

entertainment business and forgo college. Although her mother discouraged her from pursuing a profession in music, Ziegler became a
producer and songwriter and even wrote a number one song in
1975, entitled "Time Moves On." She had her own production company and during the disco era created "disco bells," in which
dancers wore chimes to create special effects. "People in New York
would never think of me as a professor PhD," she said.[15] "I used to
tell my students I'm 25 percent teacher and 75 percent entertainer."

Ziegler was introduced to technology through music and entertainment. She created an 18-in. electrical guitar and other musical
instruments. For a period, she taught the hearing impaired to sing
and play music by observing technology that was being used in a
hospital.

Ziegler firmly caught the technology bug when she was at college,
earning a bachelor's degree from Baruch College, City University of
New York; a master's degree in radio and television from Southern
Illinois University (SIU) at Carbondale; and a doctorate in higher
education and academic, and administration from SIU.[16,17] Her dis-
sertation, presented in 1984, was on broadcasters and academics,
and forecasts for future technologies.

For 3 years, Ziegler served as associate director of research, development, and technology at the University of Tennessee (UT) under
the Office of the Chancellor. For her service, she received the
Chancellor's Research and Creative Award. At UT, Ziegler coauthored with Paul Davis a national report recommending major
changes in training for broadcast journalists.[18] Jane Pauley, NBC
reporter and news anchor, provided funding for the study and
served as honorary chairperson of the task force. Among the report's
recommendations was the development of a model curriculum for
college and university broadcasting departments. Pauley funded the
effort because of concerns about the quality of undergraduate mass
communications programs. Ziegler became the first and only African
American elected to serve as president of UT's Faculty Senate.

Before joining the faculty at FAMU, Ziegler served for 1 year as
assistant professor of mass communication at Jackson State University. In 1985, she became an assistant professor, and eventually full
professor of broadcasting at UT, Knoxville. Her service in broadcasting and educational technology at UT led to her appointment as professor and Garth C. Reeves, Sr. Eminent Scholar Chair of Excellence,
in the School of Journalism and Graphic Communication at FAMU
from 1997 to 1998. In 1998, she became assistant vice president for

Academic Affairs for Educational Technology, which included the Instructional Media Center, FAMU-TV, and distance learning.

She is the recipient of research grants from Funding Exchange Network for the project Linking Communities Together: Using Home Pages for the Dissemination of Information, and another from the U.S. Department of Education's Fund for the Improvement of Postsecondary Education to develop a series of videos on race relations.

Ziegler is a member of the Society for Professional Journalists, Broadcast Education Association, Kappa Tau Alpha Honor Society, Golden Key Honor Society, and Phi Kappa Phi Honor Society. Following her appointment as acting vice president for Sponsored Research and director of University Planning and Analysis at FAMU, on August 8, 2002, Ziegler assumed an administrative assignment as assistant vice president of Instructional Technology and Academic Affairs.

NOTES

1. "Bush reappoints tech leader to virtual school." (2004, February 8). *The Tallahassee Democrat.* Retrieved July 3, 2005, from http://www.tallahassee. com/mld/democrat/news/local/7902259.htm.

2. *Florida Virtual School and Florida A&M University team up to train teachers in use of online FCAT materials.* (2003, February 21). Retrieved July 3, 2005, from the Florida Virtual School Web site: http:// www.flvs.net/_about_us/pr_famupartner.htm.

3. *Digital Divide Council unveils new statewide digital divide council clearing house.* (2002). Retrieved July 3, 2005, from the Digital Divide Council Web site: http://www.digitaldividecouncil.com/digitaldivide/ unveils_clearinghouse.html.

4. *PowerUp Florida access points.* Retrieved July 3, 2005, from ITFlorida Web site: http://www.itflorida.com/wb2/itfl/itfl_PowerUP_Florida_Access_ Points.

5. Simon, K. (2002, September 22). Award helps launch tutorial. *The Famuan.* Retrieved June 29, 2005, from http://www.thefamuanonline. com/media/paper319/news/2002/09/22/News/Award.Helps.Launch.Tutorial-278955.shtml.

6. Dhyana Ziegler, personal communication, October 14, 2004.

7. American Association for the Advancement of Science. (n.d.). *Science and everyday experiences: Importance of science literacy.* Retrieved July 3, 2005, from http://www.aaas.org/news/releases/2002/0620see3.shtml.

8. *Delta Sigma Theta and DREF implement SEE.* Retrieved July 3, 2005, from the Science and Everyday Experiences Web site: http://www.deltasee. org/index.htm.

9. *Delta SEE radio.* Retrieved July 3, 2005, from the Science and Everyday Experiences Web site: http://www.deltasee.org/radio/.

10. "Sorority launches science technology radio show." (2003, June 5). *Black Issues in Higher Education.* Retrieved July 3, 2005, from http://www.findarticles.com/p/articles/mi_m0DXK/is_8_20/ai_103563690.

11. Dhyana Ziegler, personal communication, October 14, 2004.

12. Dhyana Ziegler, personal communication, October 14, 2004.

13. Dhyana Ziegler, personal communication, October 14, 2004.

14. Dhyana Ziegler, personal communication, October 14, 2004.

15. Dhyana Ziegler, personal communication, October 14, 2004.

16. Yeager, M. (2003, February 26). Women take top two jobs at FAMU. *The Tallahassee Democrat*, p. B1.

17. Florida Agricultural & Mechanical University, Office of Public Affairs. (2002, August 22). *Ziegler appointed acting vice president for sponsored research and director of university planning and analysis.* Retrieved July 3, 2005, from http://www.famu.edu/about/admin/vppa/News/Zeigler/zeigler.html.

18. University of Tennessee. (1996, September 26). *UT's Ziegler authors national broadcasting report.* Retrieved July 3, 2005, from http://pr.tennessee.edu/news/sept96/pauley.htm.

PART IV
Cybercommunity Developers

Since the establishment of the American information infrastructure, technology has impacted more than our ability to educate young people. The impact of economic and social development within communities has never been more profound. Even the way in which we conceive of communities has changed. Community once meant physical streets and houses, schools, churches, and other structures and institutions in real space. The Internet allows us to have similar structures in cyberspace and to access these virtual communities to enhance our lives in traditional communities. African Americans are leaders in working with traditional communities to make sure that citizens are actively using these new technologies and in developing communities in cyberspace that service Black people in America. Drs. Alan Shaw, Jabari Simama, and Abdul Alkalimat are cybercommunity developers featured in Part IV.

Dr. Alan Shaw's concept of *social constructionism* was the basis for his computer networking software, MUSIC (Multi-User Sessions in Community), a tool for developing local forums and promoting discussion of community issues and for organizing and managing neighborhood-based programs and social activities (or social constructions). It has been used to develop neighborhood-based community networks in Boston, MA, and Newark, NJ.

Dr. Jabari Simama is a champion of digital literacy among Atlanta residents. One method that he used to support his cause was the Cyber Bus, a traditional bus transformed into a computer lab that could be driven to communities throughout Atlanta so that disadvantaged residents could access the information infrastructure.

Dr. Abdul Alkalimat is the creator of cyberspace communities where African Americans can research and study their history and culture. Moderated by Alkalimat, H-Afro-Am is the largest African American studies community on the Internet. Launched in 1998, H-Afro-Am currently has more than 1,000 subscribers from 25 countries.

Chapter 16

Dr. Alan Shaw

President, Imani Information Systems, and Executive Director, Linking Up Villages

NEIGHBORHOODS ARE STILL IMPORTANT IN A DIGITAL WORLD

Former Vice President Al Gore coined the term *information super-highway*[1] to promote his vision of a seamless web of communications networks, computers, databases, and consumer electronics that puts vast amounts of information at the fingertips of Americans. Toward this end, he introduced the concept of a national information infrastructure (NII) to connect classrooms, libraries, hospitals, and clinics and global information infrastructure (GII) to connect global information and communication systems worldwide.[2]

Alan Shaw has expanded on Gore's vision, extending the concepts of the NII and the GII to focus on neighborhoods. He believes that the same technology used in the NII and the GII can be used to help local communities create their own neighborhood information infrastructures.

Using Gore's analogy, Shaw stated that interstate highways would not be very useful were it not for off-ramps: "People need to travel on local byways and between blocks of houses, not just from city to city. In fact, people spend most of their time traveling along their local roadways. So, we will also need to address the issue of local infrastructure when considering the implications of the NII. In fact, many of the issues concerning social empowerment are a matter of enhancing local information infrastructure."[3–5]

Shaw produces computer networks to support neighborhood information infrastructures in cities nationwide. He began this work as a doctoral student at Massachusetts Institute of Technology (MIT) as a member of the Media Laboratory. He designed the software for a network to help members of a community rebuild a fractured social setting. He placed it in a small neighborhood in Boston and in a low-income housing development in Newark, NJ. The system has been very successful at illustrating the power of the neighborhood information infrastructure approach.[6] In addition to Boston and Newark, the system is now being used in San Francisco, CA, Baltimore, MD, and Jackson, MS, as well as Japan, Mexico, and Russia.

Turning technology inward is most important to me. People who live in neighborhoods where they don't know their neighbors can use technology to recreate a sense of community in neighborhoods. In a world where people are losing a sense of connectedness and community, people are becoming more and more isolated. Connecting with people in your own neighborhood is more powerful than connecting with people around the world, I think. If I'm connected with my neighbors, it's more likely that I make things happen in our lives. The technology affects real community and not virtual community.[7]

To carry out his efforts in neighborhoods, Shaw has started a commercial venture that develops software and a nonprofit organization that focuses on helping neighborhoods build computer systems. With Shaw as its president, Imani Information Systems develops a range of software products that focus on education, community building, and collaborative work. The company's products are Web based and are designed to build neighborhood infrastructures and information technology (IT) models.

Through Linking Up Villages, his nonprofit entity, Shaw offers Multi-User Sessions in Community (MUSIC),[8] a Web-based computer network and shared database that he developed at the MIT Media Laboratory. The system is modeled on a community-building, neighborhood-driven approach to technology that gives its users an opportunity to collaborate as they build and share virtual spaces within an online community. The MUSIC system helps local community members take charge of IT and become information managers and advocates.

Rather than relegating this technology to the experts to manage and control information on the "superhighway," MUSIC users can develop and control their own local information infrastructure, and in so doing, begin to redevelop the ties and links to one another that are critical for making "tight-knit" communities. Instead of simply providing programs, services, and information to residents or members of an organization through IT, this system seeks to make the technology a means for the users themselves to develop and produce their own programs, services, and information-gathering activities.[9]

In developing MUSIC, Shaw has taken a computer technology normally used for entertainment and recreation and adapted it for use in cities for community and neighborhood development. The MUSIC program is essentially a multiuser dungeon (MUD), which has been around for more than a decade and has become prominent on the global Internet in the past 8 years. Through MUSIC, users are able to use a MUD-like environment to coordinate and provide infrastructure to their neighborhood or community organizations.

Used mainly in computer games such as "Dungeons and Dragons," MUDs are programs that accept network connections from multiple simultaneous users and provide access to a shared database of, for example, "rooms" and "exits." Users browse and manipulate the database from "inside" the rooms, seeing only those objects that are in the same room and moving among rooms mostly via the exits that connect them. MUDs are thus a kind of social virtual reality, an electronically represented place that users can visit. MUD users can add new rooms and other objects to the database and give those objects unique virtual behavior using an embedded programming language.

MUDs generally have many users connected at the same time. All users browse and manipulate the same database and can encounter the other users and their newly created objects. MUD users can also communicate with each other in real time, usually by typing messages that are seen by all users in the same room.

MUSIC supports bulletin board postings, discussion groups, and real-time text communications among users who are logged on concurrently. There are also private places to support personal communications and proprietary information. Each account holder has a private electronic message box to send and receive text messages.

Groups of individuals can set up spaces for documents that only they are able to access. MUSIC has the mechanism for handling online voting, surveying, and polling.

Shaw has used the MUSIC program in cities nationwide. In 1995, under a program called Making Healthy MUSIC, residents of a Newark housing development with little or no computer technology experience used MUSIC to organize teen workshops, community service projects, fundraisers, and projects with Rutgers University. They have also used the technology to communicate directly with their doctors, the principal and teachers of the local elementary school, social service providers, and the local librarian as well as the local mental health association. In this case, the network is composed of computers placed in homes, social service offices, the public library, a local elementary school, Newark Public Schools central office, University of Medicine and Dentistry of New Jersey, Essex County Mental Health Association, and an area church.

MUSIC has also been used in The Signature Learning Project in San Francisco and The Algebra Project in Baltimore, Jackson, and Cambridge, MA. The Signature Learning Project (funded by AT&T and Wells Fargo) began implementing the Web-based version of MUSIC in March 1998. Fairmount Elementary School in San Francisco is educating and revitalizing its community with the Arriba Juntos Community Center, San Francisco State University, California State University, in Monterey Bay, and the San Francisco Educational Services Center. They currently have approximately 160 accounts, primarily for parents. MUSIC is also being used by the National Urban League to develop a network that enables its national office to interact more efficiently with its various sites around the country.

The Algebra Project ensures that all children, particularly those of low income and those of color, successfully complete algebra in Grade 8 and the college preparatory math sequence in high school. The MUSIC system was implemented in the Stadium School in Baltimore in fall 1997 to help students and teachers collaboratively develop curriculum. Teachers have set up rooms such as Algebra Textbook, Curriculum Resources, Credit Union, Amistad, Stories, Config/Sched/ Classes, Internet Sites, Flora and Fauna, and Recycling Club. Both students and teachers have added files to the various rooms.

In Boston, Shaw has collaborated with the Metro Boston Community-Wide Education and Information Service. In this program, a MUSIC network, "Esquare," is used by participants within various adult education programs to communicate with each other and share documents they create. Shaw also has worked with the MIT Media Lab's Boston Youth and Community Connections Program, which engages a diverse group of young people from different communities in a series of face-to-face and online activities geared to achieve a better understanding of themselves and each other. MUSIC is also being used in Boston to assist collaboration efforts for the network of Computer Clubhouses in Boston, other parts of the country, and worldwide. The Computer Clubhouse provides an after-school learning environment where young people from underserved communities work with adult mentors to explore ideas, develop skills, and build self-confidence using technology.

Access to IT, however, is not solely an issue of providing more of the networking machinery to those who are technologically marginalized. Our society must also establish methods to make IT relevant, easy, and inviting to those who have the most difficult time making their voices heard. Otherwise, fear, apathy, and ignorance will rob the underprivileged of the benefits of this technology just as readily as the lack of ownership of machinery.

By placing terminals in homes, churches, community centers, health centers, and educational institutions, MUSIC is attempting to present a model for the advancement of neighborhood infrastructure by IT as NII is also being advanced by these systems.

FUTURE EMPOWERMENT OF BLACK NEIGHBORHOODS

According to Shaw, the most devastating problems people face on a persistent basis concern local matters. He believes that the future of African Americans lies in empowering communities with networks as tools for local neighborhood development. Neighbors lead the communities in developing content, with the technology as the facilitator. Shaw emphasizes that African Americans can be not only the consumers of the technology but also the users and developers who improve the Black community:

As we give more technology to people, people become consumers with the technology. People are focused on the commercial side of the technology. They are driven by consumption. Music videos and games; that side of the technology is driving poor people. For the middle class, E-mail is the driving force that is connectedness. E-mail is missing for the poor. E-mail could be used as a forum for community development.[10]

Shaw feels that African American youth, particularly boys, should play an active role in developing the technological systems that will improve Black neighborhoods: "Young Black males could do a lot with technology. But we are not creating jobs in technology for them right now. The community should build sites and the kids should be the brilliant mind set who build the intellectual capital of the community. I am writing a book about raising Black boys because statistics are off the chart about how Black boys are failing."[11]

The Black community is in a lull between the movements, Shaw thinks. He believes the next movement will involve technology and young Black people will be involved: "Identity questions drive movements, and Black kids will find a way to identify themselves in such a way that it will drive the next movement."

The World Wide Web is pressing for connection in the outer world. There are not many projects that are working on "the village" as . . . the scope of the technology. Neighborhood is as important as everything else. The trend has been less and less attention to the community. Even in ancient times people had the commons. Today there is no commons for talking to people about neighborhood problems. The technology could push us further in that direction. If you're poor it's even worse. Your human resources are your most powerful resources. That's a real challenge for the future.

To unify neighborhoods, Shaw suggests creating community malls in which everyone can participate. These community malls would allow anyone in the neighborhood to set up wares and interact with their neighbors. He believes that the technology is available to create an economic infrastructure in neighborhoods. This would start a movement because kids would have money. The movement would be a push for a new economic infrastructure.

"NII is neighborhood information infrastructure," Shaw concluded.[12] "If you have civil rights, you could have neighborhood rights. If you have neighborhood networks, people can become citizens through their neighborhoods. Democracy can call for the neighborhood citizen to be actively involved in governing your own neighborhoods."

BIOGRAPHY

Shaw grew up in Berkeley, CA, in a world of activism. His parents hold PhDs in psychology and physics. They influenced him to understand that things done in the sciences influence people and how they think:

My mother was very involved in the black consciousness movement. Strong identity, strong commitment was the focus. This blend between the two made me think technology could make a difference in advance of issues that Black people face. This gave me a real strong appreciation for academics and focusing on working toward a doctorate. Between my parents they focused me in a direction that would lead me to addressing a lot of questions. I'm not going in the same direction as either of them, but I am strongly influenced by them.[13]

In 1985, Shaw graduated from Harvard University with a Bachelor of Arts degree in applied mathematics.[14] He received his Master of Science degree in computer science from MIT in 1988 and completed his PhD in media arts and sciences at MIT in 1995. His focus was on education, and he was part of the Epistemology and Learning Group at the Media Lab.

At MIT, Shaw pursued using technology to address issues of education, social justice, and community development. He focused his attention on dropouts and at-risk young people in the underprivileged communities of Boston. His work on MUSIC grew out of these experiences at MIT. After completing MIT, in 1998, Shaw became the technology coordinator of the Algebra Project.

He served as the co-principal investigator of the National Science Foundation's Instructional Materials Development Grant awarded to the Algebra Project for research and development of 9th-grade experiential Algebra 1 curriculum modules.

Shaw has been married to Attorney Michele Shaw since 1990. They have five children: Chinua, Yesuto, Obasi, Ima, and Ife. The Shaws jointly manage businesses, consultations with the Algebra Project, and other initiatives for community development and social justice.

NOTES

1. Office of the Vice President of the United States. (1994, December 13). *Al Gore—national information infrastructure.* Retrieved August 19, 2005, from http://clinton1.nara.gov/White_House/EOP/OVP/html/nii1.html.

2. Office of the Vice President of the United States. (1994, March 21). *Remarks—International Telecommunications Union.* Retrieved August 19, 2005, from http://clinton1.nara.gov/White_House/EOP/OVP/html/telunion.html.

3. Shaw, A., & Shaw, M. (1998). Social empowerment through community networks. In D. Schon, B. Sanyal, & W. Mitchell (Eds.), *High technology and low-income communities: Prospects for the positive use of advanced information technology.* Cambridge, MA: MIT Press.

4. Bender, W., Chesnals, P., Elo, S., Shaw, M., & Shaw, A. (1996). Enriching communities: Harbingers of news in the future. *IBM Systems Journal,* *35.* Retrieved August 19, 2005, from http://www.research.ibm.com/journal/sj/353/sectionb/chesnais.html.

5. Pinkett, R. (2000, December 5). *Making the case for technology within* *the community. From access to outcomes.* Retrieved August 19, 2005, from the Morino Institute Web site: http://www.morino.org/divides/case_post04.htm.

6. Shaw, M., & Shaw, A. (n.d.). *Linking up villages.* Retrieved August 19, 2005, from http://villagenetwork.org/LUVDescription.html.

7. Alan Shaw, personal communication, November 19, 2004.

8. Hogan, K. (1995). MoJo's October HELLRAISER. *Mother Jones.* Retrieved August 19, 2005, from http://www.motherjones.com/news/hellraiser/1995/09/hogan.html.

9. Alan Shaw, personal communication, November 19, 2004.

10. Alan Shaw, personal communication, November 19, 2004.

11. Alan Shaw, personal communication, November 19, 2004.

12. Alan Shaw, personal communication, November 19, 2004.

13. Alan Shaw, personal communication, November 19, 2004.

14. Williams, S. (n.d.) *Dr. Alan Shaw: Computer scientists of the African* *diaspora.* Retrieved August 25, 2005, from http://www.math.buffalo.edu/mad/computer-science/Dr. Shaw_alan.html.

Chapter 17

Dr. Jabari Simama
Former Director of the Office of Community Technology, City of Atlanta

BUILDING THE INFORMATION CITY

Former mayor of Atlanta Bill Campbell decided in 1999 that he could do something to close the computer gap between his city's haves and have-nots by making technology accessible to all city residents. At the time, he was also national chairman of the U.S. Conference of Mayors' Commission on Technology, so he wanted a local initiative that could be a national example.[1] "We think that this can be a model across the nation," he said. "The digital divide is not just in Atlanta. It's in every city; it's in rural communities."

In January 2000, Campbell appointed Dr. Jabari Simama, a national award-winning journalist and Georgia Tech professor, to serve as his senior public technology advisor and to direct his administration's Office of Community Technology.[2] Simama served in that position for several years and has since become vice president of the Division of Community Development at Benedict College in Columbia, SC.[3] Simama's work on Atlanta's Community Technology Initiative has become a leading prototype of methods to close the "digital divide" in cities across America.[4]

The money for the city's Community Technology Initiative came from a renegotiated contract with MediaOne, the city's cable franchisee. With $8.1 million from the cable company, Campbell started a program to bring computer access and training to as many Atlanta city residents as possible.[5] The funding was initially used to build community technology centers in city-owned buildings, schools, and libraries. Campbell named 21 corporate, educational, and community leaders to help guide the effort. The former mayor appointed Simama to oversee the development and operations of the city's community technology centers and to direct other city public and community technology initiatives.

Simama's programs reflected the city's commitment to the idea that information technology (IT) is a tool for community development. This concept included providing ways for residents to learn computing and to create and use the Web as a resource for developing strong families and neighborhoods. Under Simama, the city began to develop and maintain community portals that enabled citizens to create and use information about public services and to access these services for emergency preparedness, job opportunities, and local economic development. At the city's web portal, Atlanta citizens learned about skills and services their neighbors wanted to share with them. They also learned how to make their own skills available to their community.

Simama also brought in corporate and other strategic partners and developed cybercenters across the city. More than a dozen community cybercenters were opened primarily in low-income neighborhoods in Atlanta in community centers, recreation centers, schools, and libraries. A typical center was home to 20 to 30 computers networked and connected to the Internet via a T1 line. The cybercenters were open from 10 a.m. until 10 p.m. and offered instructor-led and online courses through Atlanta's Community Web portal. Students in the cybercenters were taught to develop much of the content for Atlanta's Community Web portal.

We have a network of 15 state-of-the-art tech centers with connectivity to the Internet in 15 distinct neighborhoods. One example is Summer Hill, a working class Black community in Atlanta where family technology training is provided, and it's intergenerational, with young and old people learning E-mail and office programs.[6]

Simama was also responsible for taking technology to the city residents even if they could not come to the cybercenters. The community technology program reached an estimated 7,000 neighborhood people, who dropped in to the various cybercenters and labs. Simama discovered, however, that "to close the digital divide, you have to get in the transportation business." Working with the current mayor of Atlanta, Shirley Franklin, Simama rolled out a project called Cyber Bus in 2001.[7] The purpose of the 40-foot computer lab on wheels was to reach more residents. Microsoft and AT&T Broadband provided the $225,000 to purchase the fully equipped vehicle. The self-powered van contains 12 flat-screen state-of-the-art computers and will be accessible by disabled people.

We have a Cyber Bus that is a technology center on wheels. It goes to areas where physical centers don't exist. Our next objective is to drive technology closer to the home. Mobility is a problem for folks who are poor. Plus there is a security problem with people being out at night. We have to drive the technology closer to the home so that it is convenient for people to use it.[8]

Through programs initiated and managed by Simama, Atlanta spent about $8 million in 5 years and about 25,000 people have used this program between 2000 and 2004. Simama believes that the program has demonstrated that low- and moderate-income city residents respond positively to high-tech programs. He believes that if resources were available, the number of labs could have been doubled and the local need still would have not been met.

If you build quality programs people will support those programs. And they won't rip off the equipment. In the low-income areas in five years of operating we had virtually no theft. This was because when you invest in people, people will respond. They respond by protecting your investment in them. Community leaders have helped to take care of the equipment. Our oldest student was 93.[9]

Cybercenters and the Cyber Bus are only some of the technological innovations that Simama brought to Atlanta. Just before leaving to take the post at Benedict College, Simama began work on a first-ever public–private partnership to build a citywide wireless Internet network.[10] It will first be established at City Hall and Hartsfield–Jackson International Airport and then rolled out to other areas around the city. Biltmore Communications, the Atlanta service provider that will build the network and manage the wireless service, already provides both wired and wireless broadband services in the area, and its wireless hotspots will eventually be integrated into the network. Wireless fidelity (Wi-Fi) is generally perceived as a kind of luxury convenience but in fact represents what will soon be the best source of broadband information access available for low-income neighborhoods. Simama initiated the effort to deploy a citywide network providing universal access to the Internet. This will be the first truly citywide network, the first led by a mayor, and the first seamless, transparent system of wireless access covering extensive indoor spaces. Called Atlanta First Pass, the network would bring benefits to the community, such as workforce development, educational enrichment, and a bridge across the digital divide, according to Simama.

MOVING FROM DIGITAL ACCESS TO DIGITAL LITERACY

Simama has always had a talent for visualizing the future and its impact on African Americans.[11] Simama sees the Black community moving beyond the digital divide to digital literacy:

I think about the digital divide the same way I think about pencils and paper. Taking technology to the community is just the beginning. It's like giving someone paper and pencil. You still have to teach people how to write. I'm not happy that the federal government is trying to withdraw funding from technology centers. What we have done so far is like giving people a pencil and paper without teaching them to write.[12–14]

Simama said that moving toward digital literacy involves investing in teachers and faculties, facilitators, and instructors who can educate the community to use computer technology. He believes that the power of the Internet is more than just access to information but one that allows people to self-publish. For Black people, he sees the opportunity to have a voice to build worldwide networks.

Simama pointed out, however, that technology does not eliminate racism because, even in an information society, everyone maintains their same identities. Discrimination in the marketplace will still occur regardless of one's technical capabilities. He added that computer technology on its own in no way eliminates social problems but it could be used as a tool for fighting racism and other social ills. Black people must develop a model of achievement that includes digital literacy in education, jobs, and the use of technology in worldwide social organizing.

It's real important that leaders who want to move their constituencies forward very much understand it as an organizing tool and that technology literacy is the other literacy. It will be as important as reading, writing, and arithmetic. Without it someone would be as handicapped as someone who couldn't read.[15]

BIOGRAPHY

Simama grew up in Columbia, MO, a town rich in journalism history. He was born Frederick Kendall Lewis and grew up in a two-room tenement with no indoor plumbing. His parents separated when Simama was 7 or 8 years old. Despite these adversities, Simama still managed to achieve at an early age and learned to play the drums by the time he was in the third grade.

Athletic and fast, Simama broke his Jefferson City, MO, high school's record for the 440-yard dash. He received a football scholarship to college and studied written composition. He later taught English composition at Atlanta Junior College in 1974 and helped the school set up its first journalism program.

After graduating from the University of Bridgeport, Simama went to Atlanta University to pursue a master's degree in African American studies. There he became involved in the Black cultural movement and took a new name: Jabari, meaning "brave," and Simama, meaning "stand up."

Simama received his doctorate from Emory University in 1978, and at age 28 he became an associate professor at Morgan State University in Baltimore, MD. In 1980 he returned to Atlanta, and Shirley Franklin, the current mayor of Atlanta, recommended him for a position at the local cable company as director of public access TV for Prime Cable (now Comcast). At this time, Atlanta had the first large urban cable system, with five studios in different neighborhoods. Simama and his colleagues spent $3.5 million and trained thousands of people to produce programs. He was the founding director and served in this position for more than 6 years. Other cities built on what Atlanta had done in cable, and it became a template for urban participation in cable.

In 1987, Simama was elected to the Atlanta City Council, where he served until 1993. He then was president pro tem of the City Council and a member of the Metropolitan Atlanta Olympic Games Authority, after being elected by his peers on the Atlanta City Council. Consistent with his commitment to collaborate and use his negotiation skills, he authored more than 300 pieces of legislation, among them a landmark ethics bill, First Source Jobs Policy, and the Georgia

Dome Stadium Community Trust Fund to rebuild the inner-city neighborhoods around the stadium.

Simama worked for many years in higher educational institutions, including Georgia Tech, University of Cincinnati, and Clark Atlanta University. He has worked 7 years in the private sector at the director level, where he established a Department of Community Access Television and Training. Moreover, he has worked as a legislator in Atlanta as a two-term city councilman, with specialties in ethics reform, communications, and leveraging City Hall to stimulate community empowerment.

From 1999 to 2004, Simama worked in the executive branch of the city of Atlanta as a cabinet-level director of marketing and communications and as an executive director of the Office of Community Technology. He has been responsible for media relations, public information, cable production operations, and telecommunications/cable franchise policy and regulatory oversight.

I always wanted to ensure that networks and systems and programs empower people and give them a voice. I was about taking technology and developing it into community media institutions to help people develop themselves and their communities. And that they have free speech. And to make sure that the community had a voice and some ownership.[16]

For 22 years, Simama, his wife, and two daughters have lived in historic Washington Park in Atlanta.

NOTES

1. Kanell, M. E. (1999, December 22). Tackling the digital divide: MediaOne will fund centers in Atlanta that will offer computer training and Internet access. *The Atlanta Journal–Constitution*. Retrieved August 27, 2005, from http://www.ajc.com/.

2. Hairston, J. B. (2000, January 8). Simama to head technology initiative. *The Atlanta Journal–Constitution*. Retrieved August 27, 2005, from http://www.ajc.com/.

3. Benedict College. (2005, April). *New vice president in the Division of Community Development*. Retrieved August 29, 2005, from http://www.benedict.edu/divisions/comdev/news/bc_community_dev_newsletter.html.

4. Post, C. (2004, September 5). Tech summit explores digital divide in cities. *Atlanta Daily World*. Retrieved August 30, 2005, from http://www.zwire.com/site/news.cfm?newsid=2148873&BRD=1077&PAG=461&dept_id=237827&rfi=6.

5. Hairston, J. (2000, March 2). City launches computer program: MediaOne gives $8.1 million to Atlanta for technology centers. *The Atlanta Journal–Constitution* Retrieved August 27, 2005, from http://www.ajc.com/.

6. Jabari Simama, personal communication, July 16, 2004.

7. Holsendolph, E. (2001, December 12). Computer on wheels: City's cyberbus brings Web to neighborhoods. *The Atlanta Journal–Constitution*. Retrieved August 27, 2005, from http://www.ajc.com/.

8. Jabari Simama, personal communication, July 16, 2004.

9. Jabari Simama, personal communication, July 16, 2004.

10. Robinson, B. (2004, May 3). *Atlanta lays out WiFi plans.* Retrieved August 30, 2005, from FCW.Com Web site: http://www.fcw.com/article86004-05-03-04-Web.

11. Mallory, M. (2002. April 10). Chief of tech center has job worth loving. *The Atlanta Journal–Constitution.* Retrieved August 27, 2005, http://www.ajc.com/.

12. Grantham, R. (2000, April 22). Georgia targets digital divide. *The Atlanta Journal–Constitution.* Retrieved August 27, 2005, from http://www.ajc.com/.

13. Holsendolph, E. (2000, June 21). Digital divide proves pesky: Atlanta's ahead of the curve nationally, but certain pockets' lack of computer skills could prove costly. *The Atlanta Journal–Constitution.* Retrieved August 27, 2005, from http://www.ajc.com/.

14. Holsendolph, E. (2001, September 2). A Georgia city decided to provide its residents with a year of free Internet access, but only half signed on: Why LaGrange isn't more wired. *The Atlanta Journal–Constitution.* Retrieved August 27, 2005, from http://www.ajc.com/.

15. Jabari Simama, personal communication, July 16, 2004.

16. Jabari Simama, personal communication, July 16, 2004.

Chapter 18

Dr. Abdul Alkalimat

Professor of
Africana Studies
and Sociology and
Director of the
Africana Studies
Program,
University of
Toledo

LINKING THE INFORMATION AGE TO THE BLACK STUDIES MOVEMENT

In the 1960s, African American college students across the nation protested the lack of academic curricula that reflected the experience of Black people in a positive way. Many of those students demanded a more relevant pedagogical approach that included the teaching of Black history and the hiring of Black faculty.[1] In 1969, Nathan Hare and Jimmy Garret at San Francisco State University organized the first Black studies program in the country. At the time, Hare said the purpose of Black studies was to motivate Black students, who were conditioned to exclusion, to have greater involvement in the educational process. For more than three decades, Black studies programs with this charge have struggled to survive at universities. Today, Dr. Abdul Alkalimat is leading a movement to bring Black studies into the Information Age by using a digitized approach: eBlack Studies.

I have been trying to conceptually link the emergence of the Information Age to the Black experience. I am rereading African American history and linking information technology advances on academic campuses to Black studies, thus eBlack Studies, moving the Black experience from the actual to the virtual.[2]

Alkalimat is professor of Africana studies and sociology and director of the Africana Studies Program at the University of Toledo. He has transformed eBlack Studies into more than just a concept. It is now a project in cyberspace that provides information for students and scholars in all academic fields that focus primarily on Africa and the African diaspora. According to Alkalimat, eBlack Studies relies on at least three theoretical concepts: (1) cyberdemocracy, maximizing potential participation; (2) collective intelligence, including all voices; and (3) information freedom, free distribution of information. Under Alkalimat's direction, eBlack Studies has five major components that fulfill the purpose of this initiative: H-Afro-Am; UG/UT Distance Learning Project; Malcolm X: A Research Site; Black Radical Congress' cyberactivity, and Cyber-Church.

Moderated by Dr. Alkalimat, H-Afro-Am is the largest African American studies discussion list on the Internet. Launched in 1998, H-Afro-Am currently has more than 1,000 subscribers from 25 countries. This moderated Internet discussion forum provides an exchange of information for professionals, faculty, and advanced students in the field of African American Studies. The forum focuses on the experience of Blacks in the United States and the African diaspora.[3] Alkalimat edits H-Afro-Am at the University of Toledo and believes that it is helping to change the way that people can become educated about people of African descent.

I began doing this type of work in the beginning in the 1990s. Since 1997 I have been editing the major listserv that deals with African Studies. It's not so much important as to what we believe but what we know. eBlack Studies.org, for example, is a Web site that includes lists of all the academic programs in Black Studies.[4]

H-Afro-Am is also the official voice of the Collegium for African American Research in Europe (CAAR). Established in 1992 by a group of European scholars, CAAR focuses on and promotes African American scholarship from an international perspective. Since its beginning, CAAR has expanded considerably and now has more than 240 members from 26 countries. The aim of CAAR is to spread information and documentation and encourage the exchange of ideas by organizing panels and conferences, publishing a newsletter, preparing collective publications, and creating working groups on a variety of topics.

The UG/UT Distance Learning Project is a partnership between the Universities of Toledo and Ghana to send courses from Africa to the world. Dr. G. K. Nukunya, professor of sociology and former University of Ghana pro vice chancellor, was a visiting professor at Toledo for the academic year 1999–2000. He taught two campus courses during the fall and the same courses via the Internet from Ghana. In this collaboration, the universities have used e-learning systems and software to teach Introduction to the African Experience and Foundations of Culture in the African Diaspora.

Information and communication technology is transforming education and that is one of the fronts of technology. But we have to look at what it is doing discipline by discipline. Little was happening in Black studies. Black studies had been based on politics and ideology. With eBlack Studies, we are attempting to move the field from ideology to information.[5]

Alkalimat has applied the principles of eBlack Studies to the study of the revolutionary leader Malcolm X. The University of Toledo had been engaged in a program of research, production, and advocacy about the life and legacy of Malcolm X since the 1960s. Alkalimat has developed one of the most authoritative sources about the revolutionary leader. Through collaboration with worldwide colleagues, Alkalimat created a Web site, "Malcolm X: A Research Site," to share information and establish an empirical baseline for studies of the slain leader. This comprehensive Web site on the life and legacy of Malcolm X is edited by Alkalimat and updated every month. The Malcolm X site gets 3,000 to 10,000 hits per day according to Alkalimat.

Malcolm X was considered a radical activist in his day. In contemporary times, Alkalimat has been reorganizing the organizational tactics of contemporary Black radicalism around the principles of eBlack Studies by collaborating with an organization called the Black Radical Congress (BRC). With this organization, Alkalimat has promoted the principle of turning ideology into information. BRC's cyberactivities have included a listserv discussion and debate, creating a "webliography" of contemporary Black radicalism, and posting official BRC documents online. Alkalimat expects to use the BRC experience as a model for other national campaigns of Black radical activists.

Alkalimat is applying eBlack Studies principles to organizations other than academic institutions and radical groups in the Black

community. He has launched a digital divide initiative that has captured the interest of hundreds of churches in the city of Toledo.[6]
Cyber-Church helps local churches go online by recruiting local
young people to train members and staff to launch Web sites. More
than 300 churches have created sites as part of the initiative.
Although the program has been most successful in the local African
American community, local synagogues and mosques are also
participating.

Cyber-Church is a Web site that focuses on religious institutions. With 500
in Toledo and 200 in Chicago and other cities. Cyber-Church has five levels:
(1) directory of church; (2) detailed church history; (3) sermons/choir; (4)
community technology center in church; and (5) Cyber-Ministry [which]
has cybercommunity in church. This will complement face-to-face interaction with the congregation rather than replace it.[7]

Alkalimat stated the goal is to get every church online via a common portal for all faiths as a virtual ecumenical environment for
Black liberation theology.

CYBERSPACE ADVANCES THE AGENDA FOR PROGRESS OF AFRICAN AMERICANS

Whether it is church or radical black organizations, Alkalimat views
the Internet as a tool for globally advancing various agendas in the
Black community. Mobilization and organization of the Black community to advance interests around education and politics are moving from "civil rights to cyberpower."[8]

Our vision is a virtual Black community. Creating this virtual world in
cyberspace is a step toward recreating the actual world we live in. eBlack
folks need a brain, and I'm talking about the kind of brain that H. G. Wells
was talking about in his book *World Brain*. That is using technology to maximize intellectual power.[9]

Alkalimat's vision for a "Black brain" includes a network that can
be used to maximize Black intellectual power. According to Alkalimat, the Black BRAIN (Black Research Archive on the Internet)[10]
would contain the papers of the 1,000 most important Black thinkers
of the last 50 years. The BRAIN could be used to get papers, to jump-
start research, and conduct searches using regular language. The
BRAIN could allow researchers to move beyond the limitations of
printed books and access texts that are usually unavailable.

This takes us beyond just the thinking of leaders. We need a way to use the distribution of information about simple things like education and health. That's how we will find ourselves mobilized in virtual movements in cyberspace. This is the first movement in history where our community has global reach and the ability to exercise power globally.[11]

Alkalimat believes that, for Blacks, the future lies in not just accessing the Internet but also actually creating new computer innovations for improving their own well-being.[12,13] Blacks can achieve this by using open source and free software. Alkalimat has been working in community centers in Toledo to create computer labs that use open source software.

Open source can allow African Americans to get in the game with less money. We need to begin to teach the youth how to write code rather than use drop-down menus. Technology is what you make it. When Black youth put their creative genius into it that will change things and the way people look at it. We need to keep putting it in people's hands. We want to raise up a new generation of people who are into freedom by using open source and free software to create their own programs. People who don't know how to use a computer will be the 21st-century version of illiterates who couldn't sign their names and marked documents with an "X" years ago. That's how serious it is.[14]

BIOGRAPHY

It is a small wonder that Alkalimat is a pioneer of the new Information Age since he is the descendant of pioneers of the antebellum frontier in America.[15–17] His relative, Frank McWorter, was a slave who purchased his own freedom and moved to Illinois. In 1836, "Free Frank," as he was called, established New Philadelphia, the first town in America founded by a Black man.

Born Gerald Arthur McWorter in 1942 in Chicago, Alkalimat grew up in Cabrini, an integrated housing development. Alkalimat stated that his family always moved by "advances of the industrial city." He went to Kansas City as a teenager, played basketball, and experienced integration at the high school level. Throughout school, he was already interested in technology and used the IBM counter sorter.

As an activist in the civil rights movement in the mid-1960s, Alkalimat was always looking for new technology. He joined the Student Nonviolent Coordinating Committee and used Watts lines to form communication networks. Alkalimat went to college and eventually received his doctorate in sociology from the University of Chicago in 1974.

He has enjoyed a distinguished career as an academician. Alkalimat published ten book-length manuscripts and many articles and has lectured throughout the world. He has published books on Malcolm X, Harold Washington, and African American history. He is a member of the editorial boards of *Information, Communication, and Society*; *cyRev: A Journal of Cybernetic Revolution*; and *Black Scholar*, for which he is a founding board member. He serves on several other editorial boards, including *Perspectives on Global Development and Technology*; *Community Information and Society*; *SAGE Race Relations Abstracts*; *Sustainable Socialism and Radical Democracy*; and *Africa World Review*.

Alkalimat has combined scholarship with activism and organization during his career. He is cofounder of several organizations, including the Institute of the Black World, National Association of Afro-American Educators, Organization of Black American Culture, African Liberation Support Committee, Peoples College, Timbuktu and Twenty First Century Books, Cooperative Research Network in Black Studies, Illinois Council for Black Studies, and the BRC.

Alkalimat continues to serve the community in which he lives. He has been the president of Toledo's W. J. Murchison Community Center,[18] a community technology center with twenty connected workstations, including printing and multimedia capability. Its mission is to educate and provide community support to alleviate the problems of underemployment, drug and alcohol abuse, and violence, and to enhance the social and economic growth of the neighborhood residents.

He is also actively involved at the national and international levels. He has organized the Technology and Employment Conferences held in Cambridge, MA, Chicago, and Los Angeles; the TH Pan-African Congress held in Zaire; and international conferences on the contributions of Malcolm X. He speaks on issues of race and class, and a new society in the context of the new technology, economy, and the end of work.

An African American studies scholar for more than thirty years, Dr. Alkalimat's most recent research on cyberspace has positioned him as an expert in the field. He has lectured at conferences and on college campuses across the United States as well as in Ghana, South Africa, Canada, and England. He was a keynote speaker at the

National Conference of the Association of College and Research Libraries in March. He also is the former director of the Afro-American Program at the University of Illinois.

NOTES

1. Hine, D. (1992, summer). The Black studies movement: Afrocentric-traditionalist-feminist paradigms for the next stage. *Black Scholar, 22,* 11–18. Retrieved August 11, 2005, from http://xroads.virginia.edu/~DRBR/hine.html.

2. Abdul Alkalimat, personal communication, September 1, 2004.

3. Alkalimat, A. (2001, October). eBlack: A 21st century challenge. *Mots Pluriels.* Retrieved August 10, 2005, from http://www.arts.uwa.edu.au/MotsPluriels/MP1901aa.html#top.

4. Abdul Alkalimat, personal communication, September 1, 2004.

5. Abdul Alkalimat, personal communication, September 1, 2004.

6. "Churches utilize cyberspace to grow links to community." (2003, April 3). *The Toledo Blade.* Retrieved August 11, 2005, from http://www.toledoblade.com/apps/pbcs.dll/section?Category=ARCHIVES.

7. Abdul Alkalimat, personal communication, September 1, 2004.

8. Alkalimat, A., & Williams, K. (2001). *Social capital and cyberpower in the African American community: A case study of a community technology center in the dual city.* Retrieved August 10, 2005, from http://www.communitytechnology.org/cyberpower.

9. Abdul Alkalimat, personal communication, September 1, 2004.

10. Alkalimat, A. *BRAIN, Black Research Archive on the Internet: Toward a research program for eBlack studies.* Retrieved August 10, 2005, from http://www.murchisoncenter.org/acrl/paper.doc.

11. Abdul Alkalimat, personal communication, September 1, 2004.

12. Alkalimat, A. (2004, April 19). Cyberorganizing. *eBlack Studies.* Retrieved August 10, 2005, from http://eblackstudies.org/grbk/organizing.pdf.

13. Williams, K., & Alkalimat, A. (n.d.). *A census of public computing in Toledo, Ohio (2002).* Retrieved August 10, 2005, from http://www.communitytechnology.org/toledo/toledo.pdf.

14. Abdul Alkalimat, personal communication, September 1, 2004.

15. University of Illinois at Urbana-Champaign. (2005, July 10). *New Philadelphia Archeology Project: Updates on project progress.* Retrieved August 10, 2005, from http://www.anthro.uiuc.edu/faculty/cfennell/NP/updates.html.

16. "Ahead of its time?" (2005, January). *Smithsonian Magazine.* Retrieved August 10, 2005, from http://www.smithsonianmag.si.edu/smithsonian/issues05/jan05/digs.html.

17. Husar, D. (2005, June 24). Free Frank leaves descendents a legacy of freedom. *Whig.com*. Retrieved August 10, 2005, from http://www. whig.com/289267086285617.php.

18. Murchison Center director fights digital divide. (2004, June 21). *The Toledo Blade*. Retrieved August 11, 2005, from http://www.toledoblade. com/apps/pbcs.dll/article?AID=/20040621/NEWS08/406210328&SearchID= 73248277638834.

PART V
Masters of the World Wide Web

During the advent of the Information Revolution, one of the greatest frontiers for Blacks has been the Internet. A 1999 U.S. Department of Commerce report, "Falling through the Net," revealed that although more Americans are using the Internet, there are far more Whites online than Blacks and Hispanics. However, there is a more encouraging picture. Some African Americans have mastered the Internet by building Web portals that not only service the Black community but also generate a profit for themselves and the operators. These Web sites have become so profitable that they too often have been taken over by major corporations that want to gain revenue from the Black consumer. Part V covers African Americans who have manipulated the Internet to their own advantage and to the benefit of the Black community at large.

Art McGee is sometimes called the Black Johnny Appleseed of the Internet. Even before the World Wide Web existed with its click on icons, McGee established a directory that African Americans could use as a resource guide to access information on the Internet geared to the Black community.

E. David Ellington and his partners created Net Noir by partnering with America On Line (AOL), one of the largest Internet service providers in the world. Ellington was a key figure among the first to turn Internet service for Black people into a strategic corporate venture.

Don Rojas's The Black World Today (TBWT) was the premiere Web portal devoted entirely to news and information for and about people of African descent. It has been described as the first daily online Black newspaper. Established in 1996, it took TBWT only 2 years to become competitive on the Internet with some of the world's leading news organizations.

Kenn Turner is largely responsible for saving two Black Web portals that might have gone under during the dotcom bubble burst. He successfully integrated them into the AOL enterprise. At AOL, he also set up marketing programs that brought more African Americans than ever before to the number one Internet service provider.

Chapter 19

Art McGee
Communications
and Technology
Consultant

IDENTIFYING A UNIQUE AFRICAN AMERICAN CYBERSPACE

In the late 1980s, it was not as easy to navigate the Internet as it is today. It was less graphically attractive, and because there was no World Wide Web, users had to have more than just a "click-on" computer capability to get around in cyberspace. The inventor of the World Wide Web, Tim Berners Lee, has stated:

Back in 1989, before the World Wide Web, many different information systems existed. They ran on different sorts of computers, each running different operating systems, connected by different networks, and using quite different programs to give to the user very different ways of accessing information.[1]

Even back then, Art McGee was already accessing information about African Americans and helping others to find Internet locations devoted to Black people. McGee is best known as the first person to create and maintain the first, and for many years the only, Black online resource directory.[2] His directory predated and led to Black Web portals that are common today.

Inspiration and philosophy are my main contributions in terms of the Internet and computing. I inspired others to think in new directions. Before there was actually the Internet, when it was ARPANET and folks were still using bulletin board systems, I began a process of going out and documenting different places where African American were using cyberspace as bulletin boards or commercial systems. This was in the early 1980s ... when I was in high school.[3]

McGee is widely regarded as a legend and is considered by many to be the father of Black or Pan-African cyberspace, having been the first person to research and document Black sociocultural production and usage in online environments. Once dubbed the Johnny Appleseed of the Internet, Art McGee is a communications and technology consultant and activist who focuses on grassroots media and communications advocacy.

Around 1980, I started compiling a directory. Around 1985, I started to compile a directory of sites that were run by African Americans and African people. I called it the Pan African Resource Guide. It started out as a personal resource. I stopped doing that in 1995 when search engines became more prominent. Search engines made these directories obsolete. They were useful when the Internet was more text based.[4]

McGee's work has been nationally recognized for its contribution to the growth and utility of the Internet. The older version of the directory has been put in a Web format and archived by University of Pennsylvania African Studies Center.[5]

The work that I did in identifying a unique African cyberspace inspired others. It made Blacks and others aware of the full presence of Africans on the Web as contributors. Others improved on it and created a cyberdiaspora that was previously invisible.[6]

DIGITAL ACTIVISM

Since creating the first directory of African American resources on the Net, McGee has continued to work as a technology and commutations specialist with organizations that seek to democratize the Internet. In the late 1990s, McGee became a technology consultant to the Black Radical Congress (BRC). He said a group of activists and academics, partially with respect to the Million Man March, established the BRC "to inject more radical discourse and to bring back a class based approach that had been part of our historical legacy and to become a countering force for racism."[7]

McGee was the coordinator of AntiRacismNet, an international network of racial justice practitioners and organizations based in Oakland, CA. AntiRacismNet is a component of the Institute for Global Communications (IGC), the world's first not-for-profit Internet service provider.[8] AntiRacismNet provides information and technical support for those interested in issues of civil rights, racism, and diversity. For antiracism advocates, this network also offers a directory of antiracism/social justice organizations, resource links, and an events calendar. The IGC played a formative role in bringing advanced communications technologies to grassroots organizations worldwide working for peace, human rights, environmental sustainability, women's rights, conflict resolution, and worker rights.

McGee is also the former technology coordinator at the Center for Third World Organizing (CTWO), a racial justice organization dedicated to building a social justice movement led by people of color. CTWO is a 25-year-old training and resource center that promotes and sustains direct action organizing in communities of color in the United States.

My work is motivated by sense of Pan Africanism and an awareness of the limitations of the electronic media to serve the needs of African Americans and Africans. I recognized a need for Black people to talk directly to each other unmediated. From the beginning I saw the Internet as a tool of liberation for Black people.[9]

USING TECHNOLOGY FOR LIBERATION

McGee feels that open source software is the key to the success of African Americans in the future. Open source software generally denotes that the source code of computer software is open to study, change, and improvement of its design through the availability of its source code under an open source license. Open source software generally allows anybody to make a new version of the software, port it to new operating systems and processor architectures, share it with others, or market it. The advantage of open source is to let the product be more understandable, modifiable, duplicatable, or simply accessible while still very marketable.

Open source holds some potential in getting way from simple consumerism and consumption of technology so that African Americans can produce some technological solutions. Hardware is more difficult because you need a factory. Africans and African Americans trained on software also reduces the cost of constantly having to upgrade to new software. So the open source movement holds promise. Different organizations are trying to get this done. This is a slowly emerging process. It is beginning but it needs to become more comprehensive.[10]

McGee sees open source and similar software as the issues for the future. He feels that more people are looking at cooperative processes that are non-market oriented, where there are shared resources in a public domain while corporations are seeking to lock down their software copyrights.[11] McGee said, "We need law and policy to be developed that complements the development of software and to put out the idea that human rights are more important than property rights."

McGee believes that African Americans will survive as consumers, but they need to produce their own information technology products. "We have a production problem, i.e., creating something for self," he said. "We need to be producing more engineers and scientists. The cotton gin was the first Information Age. This Information Age is just ramping it up. It is primarily economic issues and not so much race and culture. Black people take to technology so it's not race."

McGee feels that the "digital divide" is just a by-product of all the other divides that have existed between the haves and have-nots in America. "It doesn't necessarily exist on its own," he said. "It's new but it's also a part of existing divides. We must address the others, such as poverty, or else you are not going to get far with a digital component."

BIOGRAPHY

McGee was born and raised in Los Angeles by his father. He was a gifted student and at one time wanted to be a chemist. As time went on, he became more interested in computers and math.[12]

He left college and went into a training program and later the defense industry. He soon left the corporate environment to work in the nonprofit and small business environment. He is a communications and technology consultant with more than 15 years of experience in both the corporate and nonprofit arenas. Currently, McGee is the technology director at Media Alliance, a national media advocacy and training organization based in San Francisco, and the coordinator of AntiRacismNet, an international network of racial justice practitioners and organizations based in Oakland.

In 2000, McGee was given a Lifetime Achievement Award by Marketing Opportunities in Business and Entertainment for his pioneering work as an "Influencer & Innovator of the Internet." In 2001, McGee was named a national "New Media Hero" by the Independent Media Institute (AlterNet). McGee is currently at work on a book and film project that will explore Black people's relation to and engagement with technology from a historical, contemporary, and futuristic perspective.

NOTES

1. Lee, T. B. (2002). *The World Wide Web: Past, present, and future.* Retrieved Feb 6, 2006, from http://www.w3.org/People/Berners-Lee/1996/ppf.html.

2. McGee, A. (n.d.). *Critical cyberculture studies: Current terrains future directions.* Retrieved February 6, 2006, from the Resource Center for Cyberculture Studies Web site: http://www.com.washington.edu/rccs/ford/bios/mcgee.html.

3. Art McGee, personal communication, October 23, 2004.

4. Art McGee, personal communication, October 23, 2004.

5. African Studies Center, University of Pennsylvania. (n.d.). *Black/African related resources.* Retrieved February 6, 2006, from http://www.africa.upenn.edu/Home_Page/mcgee.html.

6. Art McGee, personal communication, October 23, 2004.

7. Black Radical Congress. (n.d.). *Forging a Black liberation agenda for the 21st century.* Retrieved February 6, 2006, from http://www.blackradicalcongress.org/index.html.

8. Institute for Global Communication. (n.d.). *About IGC.* Retrieved February 6, 2006, from http://www.igc.org/html/aboutigc.html.

9. Art McGee, personal communication, October 23, 2004.

10. Art McGee, personal communication, October 23, 2004.

11. McGee, A. (2004, August 25). *Advocating free software to non-profits?* Retrieved February 6, 2006, from http://lists.debian.org/debian-nonprofit/2004/08/msg00013.html.

12. Art McGee, personal communication, October 23, 2004.

Chapter 20

E. David Ellington
Cofounder and
Former President
and Chief
Executive Officer,
NetNoir

OCCUPYING THE FIRST BUSINESS SPACE IN CYBERSPACE

Marc Andreessen is the man who made it possible for ordinary people to get on the Internet and move around without having any special computer skills.[1] He created the Mosaic graphical browser for the Internet and World Wide Web. He also led the team that created Netscape Navigator, one of the first World Wide Web browsers for the Windows and Macintosh platforms. Andreessen has said that his creations were only the beginning and that "the single most important thing that has happened is the thousands of people [who] have created new applications using this stuff that none of us thought of or ever would have thought of."

E. David Ellington was one of the first to think about how to use the World Wide Web to serve the African American community and generate a profit at the same time. He was a key figure among the first to turn Internet service for Black people into a strategic corporate venture. In 1993, Ellington was a young entertainment lawyer who was looking for opportunities in the new media. He had been working with CD ROM for a while when he went to a computer conference and discovered that something new was coming called the World Wide Web.

I realized that there was nothing on there for Blacks. I was motivated to use Black culture and at the time no one was there. I had no idea how big it would become. I developed a business plan. I came up with the name NetNoir as something different and unique.[2]

Ellington was interested in the new media but he did not have the technological skills, so he needed a partner. Around that time, he was introduced to Malcolm Casselle, who was completing his master's degree in computer science at Stanford University, and they became friends and business partners. Through a mutual friend, they met with America On Line (AOL) president Ted Leonsis, who had announced the creation of the Greenhouse, a program to expand the areas of AOL.[3]

When Ted Leonsis became president, he announced he was looking for "infopreneurs" and was investing $10 million in people who were going to help to build this new media called the Internet. My girlfriend, who later became my wife, was working for him and she told him that I had a company, NetNoir, that was perfect for this. He said, "Okay, send me a business plan," and of course we didn't have any of that. I pulled together a group of people that I knew, and we built this plan and got it to him a month later.[4]

Leonsis thought NetNoir was a brilliant idea and provided the founders of the Black network with seed capital, in-kind support, and distribution services. On November 17, 1994, Ellington closed the deal with AOL as the first investor. AOL took 19 percent of the company for $1 million, with $300,000 in cash and $700,000 in in-kind service and AOL support in the form of placement on the Internet and promotions.

NetNoir was the first Black Web portal to have a strategic corporate investor that validated the space and the first to get venture capital and professional investors. The other two that were up and running at that time were New York Online (NYO) with Omar Wasow, who went to school with Malcolm. But NYO was like a bulletin board service. NetNoir came next and then Black Voices with Barry Cooper. What we (NetNoir) should be known for is that we validated the vertical Black Internet space by getting outside institutional money and proving that there could be a business there. NetNoir pioneered Black folks being viable on the new media. Therefore, others who came later got funding.

NetNoir, Inc. became an African American majority-owned California corporation based in San Francisco.[5] It was the leading new media company promoting, developing, digitizing, archiving, and distributing distinctive Black/urban programming and commercial applications for all forms of interactive media. NetNoir's business model had three divisions: NetNoir Multimedia Services, NetNoir Online, and NetNoir Market Research. NetNoir Online launched on June 19, 1995, because of its historical significance to the African American community.[6] In the Black community, June 19 is called "Juneteenth" and represents the date the Emancipation Proclamation was made known to the slaves in Texas, who got the word two years late.

NetNoir's online brands included editorial content, interactive communities, tools and services, and blackshopping.com, the leading retailer of Afrocentric and mainstream products. Based in San Francisco, NetNoir's investors included SynCom Ventures and Radio One. For more than five years, NetNoir was the premier Black Web portal. Then the dotcom bubble burst.[7]

I sold NetNoir in 2001. What I got out of it was operational experience for how to run a company. I learned how the venture capital industry works and I got a lot of credibility in the marketplace. I now own Blue Laser, which is a holding company for stock in companies that I invested in and participated in along the way. That's how I benefited from that. Now I am a trustee in the San Francisco Pension Fund that invests in all areas. I was appointed by Mayor Willie Brown and now I'm in the finance business leveraging the NetNoir experience. I understand [information technology] and finance from an operational perspective.[8]

USING TECHNOLOGY FOR WEALTH BUILDING

Ellington believes that one way to close the gaps between the computer haves and have-nots is to teach people use the technology for wealth building.[9,10]

I never completely bought into the idea of a digital divide. It is affecting all of humanity. It takes longer for technology to trickle down. We (African Americans) are the largest consumers of cable and we built the pager industry. When a technology makes sense to us then we are definitely integrated. So as consumers this is a non-issue. But getting employment and empowerment is a different matter.[11]

As Ellington became a successful businessman, he recognized that many people of color were not participating in the digital revolution. He saw a need in the community and began to figure out how to bring people of color and other disadvantaged Americans into the computer industry. In 1997, he met Dan Geiger, consultant to the Bay Area's Local Economic Assistance Program, who wanted to start a training program to get minorities involved in Internet businesses. Because he ran an Internet company, Ellington knew there were jobs such as managing Web sites that people could learn without a formal education.

Ellington and Geiger founded OpNet, a multimedia internship program for disadvantaged youth.[12] At OpNet, they train students for five weeks in HTML, Java scripting, and other skills and then provide them with paid four-month internships in local multimedia companies.

We've been incredibly successful in placing our interns. So far, we've had 90 students come through the program, and about 55 percent of them got long-term jobs through us. Those interns went from making $19,000 a year working at Burger King to making $35,000 or more in multimedia gulch. And none of them have a college degree.

OpNet is Ellington's method for solving the "digital divide." It creates economic opportunity for low-income young adults between the ages of 18 and 25 through technical training and career development. His strategy is to provide promising youth with the necessary information technology skills, along with the work experience, to compete in the new economy. The program trains students in both technical and job preparedness skills and then assists them in gaining paid internships or direct employment in a technology position. OpNet's program also fosters an entrepreneurial spirit in students, and many of them have gone on to form their own successful businesses.

BIOGRAPHY

Ellington received his Bachelor of Arts degree in history from Adelphi University and a Masters of Art degree in comparative politics and government from Howard University.[13] He received his Juris Doctor from Georgetown University Law Center, where he concentrated on international, corporate, and tax law. He then completed Cornell University's FALCON (Full Year Asian Language Concentration) Program in Japanese.

Ellington moved to California to practice law in Los Angeles. His firm specialized in international, entertainment, and multimedia/new technology law. At that time, he served as the chairman of the International Law Section of the Beverly Hills Bar Association. He is a member of the State Bar of California.

Ellington has extensive international business experience in Tokyo, Singapore, Bangkok, London, Dubai, and India. He has traveled around the world six times, with the longest stint being 20 months. His skill set includes asset allocation, governance, private equity, venture capital, media, entertainment law, Internet strategy, government policy, and philanthropy.

He is a charter member of TiE-Silicon Valley and a member of Business Executives for National Security and the Commonwealth Club of California and is on the board of directors of the San Francisco Jazz Organization.

Ellington has combined his business activities with service to the community. In addition to being the cofounder and chairman of OpNet, he is on the advisory board of the Center for Media Studies at Rutgers University. Among his civic activities, Ellington is commissioner of the Telecommunications Commission for the City and County of San Francisco and a member of the San Francisco Workforce Investment, the U.S. Federal Trade Commission, and the Advisory Committee on Online Access and Security.

Ellington has been recognized in *UPSIDE* magazine's Technology "Elite 100" for 1999. He received *Black Enterprise* magazine's Entrepreneurs Award as Business Innovator of the Year in 1996.

Ellington has served as president and trustee on the San Francisco Employees' Retirement System (SFERS) Board. SFERS is the fifth largest pension fund in the state of California, with $13.2 billion of assets under management. The SFERS Board also has oversight of a 457 Deferred Compensation Plan with more than $1.1 billion in assets. The SFERS's portfolio includes public equities, fixed income, real estate, and private equity. Ellington is chair of the Governance Committee and a member of the Alternative Investments Committee. He was board president from March 2003 to June 2004.

Ellington's interests include travel, yoga, vedantic meditation, tennis, sailing, and general physical exercise. He is the widower of Wendy Marx (1967–2003). He currently lives in San Francisco.

NOTES

1. Stark, T. (1995). *The Marc Andreessen interview page.* Retrieved February 7, 2006, from http://users.rcn.com/thomst/marca.html.
2. E. David Ellington, personal communication, November 19, 2004.

3. Duncan, J. (1995, January 5). *AOL greenhouse—Updated deadline*. Retrieved February 7, 2006, from http://scout.wisc.edu/Projects/PastProjects/NH/95-01/95-01-13/0005.html.

4. E. David Ellington, personal communication, November 19, 2004.

5. Ellington, E. D., & Casselle, M. (1995, November). How we did it: NetNoir, Inc. *Essence*. Retrieved February 7, 2006, from http://www.looksmartparents.com/p/articles/mi_m1264/is_n7_v26/ai_17649301.

6. The Graduating Engineer. (n.d.). *E. David Ellington interview*. Retrieved February 7, 2006, from http://www.graduatingengineer.com/articles/minority/1-17-00.html.

7. Black Web Portal Newswire. (2001, January 12). *Black dotcom shake up*. Retrieved February 7, 2006, from http://www.blackwebportal.com/wire/DA.cfm?ArticleID=108.

8. E. David Ellington, personal communication, November 19, 2004.

9. Ellington, E. D. (2000, April 1). *Giving resources to create wealth*. Retrieved February 7, 2006, from the Kauffman Foundation Web site: http://www.inc.com/articles/2000/06/19899.html.

10. Rosenfeld, J., & Ellington, E. D. (1999, December 30). Giving back. *Fast Company*. Retrieved February 7, 2006, from http://pf.fastcompany.com/magazine/30/one.html.

11. E. David Ellington, personal communication, November 19, 2004.

12. OpNet. (n.d.). *OpNet community ventures*. Retrieved February 7, 2006, from http://www.opnetwork.org.

13. "E. David Ellington." (2000, April 17). Retrieved February 7, 2006, from http://www.geocities.com/edavidellington.

Chapter 21

Don Rojas
Founder and
Former Chief
Executive Officer,
The Black World
Today

BRINGING NEWS TO THE BLACK WORLD VIA THE INTERNET

The International Academy of Digital Arts and Sciences (IADAS) was founded in 1998 to help drive the creative, technical, and professional progress of the Internet. In the same year, The Black World Today (TBWT) was a nominee for the Webby, the leading honor for Web sites and individual achievement in technology and creativity presented by IADAS.[1] According to *The New York Times*, "Good Morning America," and even the BBC, the Webbys are equivalent to the Oscars in the film industry. Awards are given in several categories every year, and in each category the IADAS selects five nominees and one winner from hundreds of entries. In 1998, TBWT was one of the five nominees in the category of "Politics and Law." The winner in that category was CNN.

At that time, TBWT was the premiere Web portal devoted entirely to news and information for and about people of African descent. It has been described as the first daily online Black newspaper. Don Rojas established TBWT in 1996, and after 2 years it was competitive on the

146

Internet with one of the world's leading news organizations. As the founder and chief executive officer (CEO), Rojas aimed to make TBWT a multimedia communications company dedicated to the reporting and dissemination of relevant news, views, and useful information about people of color communities around the world.[2] TBWT offered a host of informational and entertainment services, including national and international news, sports, commentaries, audio content, job and career listings, music, weather, shopping, and distance learning. TBWT fostered interaction and community involvement among its many users through text and audio chat, bulletin boards, letters to the editors, public opinion polls, and free classified ads. It also published reader-written reviews of books, movies, music, theater, and art exhibits. TBWT is read and listened to in more than 70 countries around the world and receives about 250,000 unique visits each month.[3]

In 1999, Rojas was named one of the "Silicon Alley dozen," a group of Internet CEOs pioneering new media developments in New York City. Writers and correspondents for The Black World Today have won several journalism awards, including first-place honors in a number of categories in the 2000 Awards of the New York Association of Black Journalists.

THE NEW PARADIGM FOR BLACKS AND TECHNOLOGY

We tried to create a new paradigm with TBWT from an Afrocentric per-spective and use technology to present it. We have had to take some heavy blows because the marketplace was not ready for it back then. Many of the pioneers have gone out of business or been bought up. Black Voices was bought by AOL Time Warner, NetNoir is gone, and BET.com is now owned by Viacom. Those that were independent and don't have big backers have bitten the dust or been gobbled up.[4]

Despite its high quality of journalism, TBWT had a difficult time on the Internet because it was never able to get the financial support it needed to be prosperous.[5] TBWT had no promotional budget and became known to African American Web users solely by word of mouth. The site got 250,000 hits with an estimated 50,000 regular readers. Seventy percent were college educated, were in their 30s to 50s, and earned more than $55,000/year. Nevertheless, the financial backers never flocked to the site.

Rojas dreamed of finding venture capital to build an independent international news organization. So he approached dozens of venture capitalists around the country and was turned down by every firm and fund he approached. Despite the rough times, TBWT has survived the bursting of the Internet bubble and the takeover of Black Web portals by major corporations. Today it is a nonprofit, reader-supported entity that continues to report the news to people of African descent in America and worldwide.

It is not surprising that Rojas has maintained TBWT while other Web portals have gone under or been bought up. Rojas feels that Blacks must own more hardware and software companies as well as companies that produce content for the Internet. He believes that although Black people are consuming products of information revolution at a very high rate, they are not making as much progress as they should in ownership of companies and patents.

The digital divide is being chipped away and 4 or 5 years from now will be minimal at best. This is because the digital divide is defined by economic power to own a computer connected to the Internet. The digital revolution has developed to the point where you will be able to connect to the Internet with a number of devices with a number of instruments that have nothing to do with a computer sitting on a desk; like cell phone, Blackberry, or PDA. In the next couple of years, the prices of these devices will be affordable. Even PC prices are going down. The younger generation is very comfortable with new technologies. In 4 to 5 years the digital divide will be a moot issue.[6]

PIONEERING BLACK INTERNET RADIO

In the meantime, Rojas has moved on to become a pioneer of Internet radio. In December 2002, he became general manager of WBAI Pacifica Radio, the New York metropolitan area's premier community radio station.[7] In that capacity, Rojas supervised a staff of more than 230 producers, journalists, engineers, and administrators. He was responsible for all aspects of programming, policy, personnel, new media, and finance.

Among his many accomplishments at the station, Rojas upgraded the station's technological infrastructure, redesigned its Web site with revenue-generating e-commerce and Internet radio features, and launched a station e-newsletter. While he was general manager, WBAI streamed the station's programming over the Internet to people all over the world. Rojas believes that Internet radio is important because of its worldwide audience and that the Internet will transform radio as we know it.

We launched a virtual Pacifica Station in August 2004. We had over 5,000 registered users in the nation and all over the world. That is radio for the future. This is a pioneering effort because we are programming for the Web. We are focusing on developing content that has universal appeal. We have to use a global scheduling clock. This type of radio is interactive across the world. We archive selected programs so that listeners can listen to them whenever they like. This is an empowering opportunity.[8]

Since then, Rojas has moved on from WBAI to take on a new project in Internet radio. His new mission is to use the Internet as a medium for connecting Caribbean nations with Caribbean diaspora communities. He has joined Dr. Karl Rodney, publisher of the New York *CaribNews* to establish Carib World Radio, a joint venture between *CaribNews* and TBWT.[9] The site's goal is to become the leading Internet radio station and online newspaper for Caribbean diaspora communities. Besides the Caribbean focus, a vital part of the mission of Carib World Radio is to facilitate communications and collaborations between the Caribbean diaspora communities and the Black world diaspora communities of North America, Europe, Latin America, and Africa.

What excites me now in my career is satellite and Internet radio and Black world audiences. We are an oral people. Black radio is the most influential of all media in the Black community because we are oral and we listen. If you transfer this to a technology platform, I think the possibilities are mind-blowing.[10]

BIOGRAPHY

Rojas was born and raised in Saint Vincent in the Caribbean. His father was a broadcaster. In the 1960s, Rojas went to the University of Wisconsin on a scholarship and afterward worked as a journalist. He served the National Urban League as its assistant director of communications for two years and later became assistant editor of the *Baltimore Afro-American* newspaper.[11] From 1979 to 1983, he worked in Grenada, West Indies, as the editor-in-chief of the national newspaper and as the press secretary to Prime Minister Maurice Bishop. In the mid-1980s, Rojas worked in an executive position at the International Organization of Journalists in Prague, Czechoslovakia. There he was responsible for servicing affiliated journalists and media workers' groups throughout North America and the Caribbean.

In the 1990s, Rojas continued his work as a journalist and manager. He served as executive editor and assistant to the publisher of the *New York Amsterdam News*. He also worked as a consultant to several media organizations, labor unions, and the National Council of Churches.

Rojas has also taught courses on the history of journalism and on minorities in the media at Long Island University's School of Journalism. He has written opinion pieces in several major publications, such as *Essence* magazine and *US Newsday* newspaper. He has edited four books of speeches and documents from the Grenadian and Cuban revolutions.

Rojas has been an organizer and activist among journalists on the international scene. He coordinated the first-ever regionwide conference of Caribbean journalists and the first-ever conference of Caribbean intellectuals, both of which were successfully convened in Grenada in 1981 and 1983. He also organized the first fact-finding tour of a delegation of African American journalists to the Soviet Union, East Germany, and Czechoslovakia in the summer of 1985. Rojas was the only Black journalist from the United States to report on the first summit meeting between Presidents Ronald Reagan and Mikhail Gorbachev in Geneva, Switzerland, in 1985.

NOTES

1. "Establishing Nominees, Winners and Webby Worthy sites." (n.d.). Retrieved February 6, 2006, from the Webby Awards Web site: http://www.webbyawards.com/webbys/index.php.
2. "The Black World Today launches largest portal for African American businesses, organizations and churches." (1999, November 1). Retrieved February 6, 2006, from the Exodus On-line Web site: http://www.exodusnews.com/NATIONAL/national058.htm.
3. The Black World Today. (2003, November 4). *Welcome to the new TBWT.* Retrieved February 6, 2006, from http://www.tbwt.org.
4. Don Rojas, personal communication, October 31, 2004.
5. Ward, J. (1999, July 12). Outside looking in. *The Industry Standard.* Retrieved February 6, 2006, from http://www.thestandard.com/article/0,1902,5426,00.html.
6. Don Rojas, personal communication, October 31, 2004.
7. Pacifica Radio. (2002, November 27). *Pacifica Radio appoints Don Rojas to lead WBAI 99.5 FM in New York.* Retrieved February 7, 2006, from http://www.pacifica.org/news/021127_newWBAIGM.html.
8. Don Rojas, personal communication, October 31, 2004.
9. Carib World Radio. (n.d.). Mission statement. Retrieved February 6, 2006, from http://www.caribworldradio.com/mission.php.
10. Don Rojas, personal communication, October 31, 2004.
11. MOBE.com. (2002). *Marketing opportunities in business and entertainment.* Retrieved February 7, 2006, from http://www.mobe.com/next/bio/iiit_drojas.html.

Chapter 22

Kenn Turner
Former Senior Vice President and General Manager, America On Line Key Audiences

SAVING THE BLACK DOTCOMS

In 2000, a new technological millennium began, but commerce on the Internet took a turn for the worse. The dotcom bubble burst, and speculative investors lost hundreds of millions of dollars as many Internet companies folded. Most business analysts would say that the crash was due to extremely overinflated technology stocks. They were inflated because, before the burst, too many companies with a "dotcom" in their names received venture capital and were quickly pushed to an initial public offering on the stock market. These companies often failed because of ill conceived and poorly executed business plans. The dotcom explosion left a trail of bankrupt companies, hundreds of thousands of people out of work, and an entire business sector in a tailspin.

Around the same time, there was much discussion about whether or not African Americans were even accessing the Internet and supporting Internet commerce in the first place. It was assumed that many African Americans were stuck on the wrong side of the digital divide. Under these conditions, one would expect that Internet companies that were geared to Black users would have gone the way of most dotcoms that blew up during this economic tragedy.

Instead of failing, two Internet portals that were popular in the Black community overcame the odds and were integrated into one of the largest Internet businesses in the world. Kenn Turner is largely responsible for saving Africana.com and Black Voices and successfully merging them into the America On Line (AOL) enterprise. At AOL, he also set up marketing programs that brought more African Americans than ever before to the number one Internet service provider. Turner's Internet experience began when he was the chief executive officer (CEO) at Africana.com before he became an executive at AOL.

I came to Africana in the winter of 2000. I joined a month before the Internet bubble burst in March 2000. We raised $3.2 million in venture capital. And we planned to raise $30 million by the summer. But how do you raise that kind of money when people are deserting the Internet like roaches when you cut the light on.[1]

Africana.com was cofounded in January 1999 by Harvard University educators Drs. Henry Louis Gates, Jr., Kwame Anthony Appiah, and Harry M. Lasker, III, to enhance educational and economic opportunities for Blacks in America and worldwide.[2] Lasker was one of the developers of the popular children's program "Sesame Street," and the partner in Africana.com who provided much of the financial support for the initial effort. Earlier, Gates and Appiah had written the *Africana Encyclopedia* and were working on the African Encarta Reference Suite with Microsoft Corporation.

They built the Africana Web site in about a year using an Israeli firm out of Tel Aviv. They used Koret Communications for management and back-end services and they used Harvard students for the writers and editors. By 1999 they were talking about taking the firm public so they needed to raise money. They needed professionals to go out and raise money.[3]

Recruited by Lasker, Turner became the CEO of the upstart firm and led the management team that positioned Africana.com to be sold to AOL. In 2000, the Time Warner Company, owner of AOL, acquired Africana.com from Gates, Appiah, and other investors.[4]

What I'm proud of is that Africana.com should have dried up and died but it didn't. The management team, the founders and the staff worked very hard with a venture capital firm from Boston to package the company in such a way that we sold it to Time Warner. It was the only company they bought during the time that they were talking to AOL. We took this tiny little high-brow, definitely intellectual, Web site that wasn't about entertainment. It was an Internet site for grownups ... We were the only stand-alone adult site out there talking about issues relevant to Black people like crime, poverty, careers, financial wealth, health, and religion.[5]

After the merger of Africana.com and AOL, Turner was hired by AOL and soon became the company's senior vice president and general manager of AOL Key Audiences. He was responsible for setting the strategy and managing AOL's emerging businesses. These businesses included the African American programming group Africana.com, BlackVoices.com, and AOL Black Focus, AOL Latino, and AOL for Small Business.

MERGING AFRICANA.COM AND BLACK VOICES AT AOL

Turner was one of the key individuals responsible for making AOL successful in the Black community. Acquiring Africana.com was only one part of AOL's a long-term strategy to make it the brand of choice in the African American community.[6] In 2003, AOL launched Black Focus, a special content area for African Americans, in a bid to better serve one of the fastest growing segments of the online audience. Around that time, USA Today reported that Blacks made up about 4 million (14%) of AOL's 27 million U.S. members.[7] At that time, AOL had offered Black-oriented chat rooms and message boards but only limited content. Black online users were expected to grow at an 8.4 percent rate from 2004 to 2007, twice that of the White audience. AOL researchers also said Blacks were 27 percent more likely than the general audience to get a broadband Internet connection in the next year and read online ads. In February 2004, under Turner's direction, AOL merged Africana.com with BlackVoices, a site that AOL had acquired from the Tribune Company.

We saved Africana.com, integrated it into AOL, and launched Black Voices last year. We spent zero dollars on marketing and through word of mouth became the number two Web site for Blacks on the Internet.[8]

EXPANDING BLACK PARTICIPATION ON THE INTERNET

In August 2004, Turner and AOL moved to get more African Americans and other minorities onto their service. AOL launched the Optimized PC, an affordable computer system that included the hardware and software needed to get consumers up and running and online.[9] Available for $299.99 with a 12-month AOL membership commitment of $23.90 a month, the AOL Optimized PC was sold in Office Depot stores and in other major retail locations nationwide. Turner recognized that this effort would allow more Blacks to get online because it reduced the cost of purchasing and operating a computer. He did not see it as a remedy for closing the digital divide in the Black community.

The digital divide is more relevant today than it was when the term was coined.[10] Blacks still lag significantly behind when it comes to Internet penetration. It's a big problem in the Information Age. When technology determines who succeeds and who fails, he who understands technology and the Internet is empowered. He who doesn't is screwed. You either get it or you don't.

The AOL Optimized PC was preloaded with the software consumers need to enjoy their PC experience. For bilingual households, the AOL Optimized PC made it easy to select and switch between language preferences. Although billed as the computer for the first-time computer user, this package was evidently designed to get more Blacks and Hispanics online because they represent growth markets for the Internet. This effort was so popular that AOL has since announced that "We are sorry, but this special AOL offer is now sold out and is no longer available."[11]

Blacks are at 35 percent while it's 70 percent for Whites. We are ahead of Hispanics. Black birth rates are two times that of Whites and Hispanics are seven times that of Whites. So as you project Internet penetration, what all of the indicators show us is that by 2008–2009 White folks and Asians will plateau at about 72 percent and Black and Hispanics will reach about 65 percent. This is the closing of the gap. The digital divide is still relevant but you don't hear about it because the current administration doesn't care about it. Digital divide was a construct that was brought forth for discussion by the Clinton Administration because you had Blacks who drove the issue. In this administration you have no Blacks who are driving the issue.[12]

Turner believes that Black people need a new model of achievement. He feels that civil rights depended on changing laws and that more African Americans should go into business and corporations.

We live in a world of great transitions. You can be afraid of that transition and grovel in fear and be ignorant and be detached and let it trample you. Or you can embrace it and accept that change is messy and unpredictable.

You have to be able to embrace change and believe that you will have positive results. But you have to be prepared. A whole lot of it is luck. But you've got to be good.

BIOGRAPHY

As the eighth of ten children, Kenn Turner spent his life in pursuit of excellence. He was born in Louisiana and his parents were rural farmers. Born Leroy Hill, Jr., he changed his name to Kenneth Leroy Turner his freshman year of college out of respect for his stepfather, who was the only father he ever knew. His family was a military clan. His father fought in Korea and his oldest brother joined the Marines in 1956 and was part of the first group to go to Viet Nam. His other siblings were also in the military.

Turner earned a Bachelor of Science degree at Southern University, Baton Rouge, LA. An NROTC scholarship midshipman in college, Turner received a regular commission in the U.S. Navy, where he served in the submarine service on active duty for seven years.[13] During the 1980s, he completed various assignments, including assistant nuclear weapons officer onboard USS *Stonewall Jackson* and taught at the Naval Guided Missiles School. Turner resigned his active commission in 1987 and transferred to the U.S. Naval Reserves, where he currently holds the rank of captain and is assigned to the office of the Chief of Naval Operations at the Pentagon.

After active duty, Turner went to work for Hallmark Cards, Inc., in the late 1980s and became business marketing manager of Alternative Cards and Stationery. Assuming roles of increasing responsibility during his 8-year tenure, Turner completed stints in executive development, new product development, new business strategy, and brand management. He was also instrumental in the development of Hallmark's first ever African American-oriented line of greeting cards: Mahogany.

I interviewed with Hallmark Cards and they offered me a job. They offered my fiancée a job too. It became a package deal and we went off to Hallmark in 1987. I went into the executive training program and was the only Black in the class. I was in training for a year and a half and then I went into marketing.

He launched personalized greeting cards that allowed people to design their own cards and put in their own message. He also managed the Alternative Cards and Stationery at Hallmark, which was about $50 to 60 million worth of responsibility.

Before joining AOL, Turner worked for Hasbro Toys, Inc. During his 5-year tenure, he led various product development and brand management efforts, including the U.S. regional marketing team and the company's Trade Marketing Departments. In January 1995, he became head of Activity Toys and managed about $140 million worth of business.

NOTES

1. Kenn Turner, personal communication with Spencer Hamilton, summer 2005.

2. Holland, R. (2001, April 21). Africana.com aims to unite a global web community. *Boston Business Journal*. Retrieved February 7, 2006, from http://www.bizjournals.com/boston/stories/2000/04/24/story6.html.

3. Kenn Turner, personal communication with Spencer Hamilton, summer 2005.

4. "Where's Africana? The end of Black online independence." Retrieved February 7, 2006, from the BlackState.com Web site: http://www.blackstate.com/blacksites.html; "Time Warner acquires Africana.com." (2000, September 8). *The Write News*. Retrieved February 7, 2006, from http://www.writenews.com/2000/090800_timewarner_africana.htm.

5. Kenn Turner, personal communication with Spencer Hamilton, summer 2005.

6. "Where's Africana? The end of Black online independence." Retrieved February 7, 2006, from the BlackState.com Web site: http://www.blackstate.com/blacksites.html.

7. Davidson, P. (2003, May 28). AOL to launch area for African-Americans. *USA Today*. Retrieved February 7, 2006, from http://www.usatoday.com/money/media/2003-05-27-aol-black-focus_x.htm.

8. Kenn Turner, personal communication with Spencer Hamilton, summer 2005.

9. Time Warner. (2004, August 12). *America Online, Inc. introduces the AOL(r) optimized PC*. Retrieved February 7, 2006, from http://www.time warner.com/corp/newsroom/pr/0,20812,681096,00.html.

10. Kenn Turner, personal communication with Spencer Hamilton, summer 2005.

11. America On Line. (n.d.). *Introducing the AOL optimized PC*. Retrieved February 8, 2006, from http://www.aolcheckout.com/aol-pc/aol_01.asp.

12. Kenn Turner, personal communication with Spencer Hamilton, summer 2005.

13. "Kenn Turner, Chief Executive Officer." (2003). Retrieved February 7, 2006, from http://cache.zoominfo.com/CachedPage/?archive_id=0&page_id= 821322396&page_url=www1%2Eafricana%2Ecom%2Fabout%2Fstaff% 2Fmanagement%2Easp&page_last_updated=12%2F12%2F2004+6%3A17% 3A18+AM&firstName=Kenn&lastName=Turner.

PART VI
Chief Executive Officers, Entrepreneurs, and Big Money Makers

In the later stages of the Information Revolution in America, two things occurred that seemed to be contradictory. According to researchers and political–social pundits, African Americans were falling behind in the race to access the technology of the information infrastructure and at risk of becoming digitally illiterate in the age of information. On the other hand, many African Americans not only became masters of the Internet but also became industry leaders in mainstream companies and in companies that they built from the ground up. Part VI covers the second group: Black corporate and entrepreneurial chief executive officers (CEOs) who lead the Information Revolution in America and the rest of the world.

Richard D. Parsons became CEO and chairman of the board of the greatest Internet and media conglomerate in the history of electronic communications. He led AOL Time Warner through a turbulent merger to become a stable, profitable enterprise that is in the forefront of the Information Revolution.

John W. Thompson took over an antivirus software firm in Silicon Alley and turned it into a corporate entity to be reckoned with in the information technology industry. He turned Symantec from a $632 million consumer software company to a $1.2 billion enterprise security market leader. He was tapped by President George W. Bush to provide advice on how to keep the nation's information infrastructure safe and secure in the time of cyberterrorism.

Over the past couple of decades, Robert L. Johnson built BET Holdings, Inc., the largest Black-owned media company that America had ever seen. Then he decided to use the technology of the Information Revolution to expand his media empire even further. He launched a portal for African Americans, making BET the number one Black location on the Web, and tied much of his BET programming to the digital cable television tier, increasing his audience and profits.

Noah Samara founded WorldSpace to provide digital satellite audio, data, and multimedia services primarily to the emerging markets of Africa and Asia. Unlike many other media moguls, he is running his business as a social cure as well as to make money. Most of his WorldSpace projects are focused on providing people in disadvantaged parts of the world with information that will help them to improve their quality of living.

Chapter 23

Richard D. Parsons

Chairman and
Chief Executive
Officer, Time
Warner, Inc.

MERGING THE OLD MEDIA WITH THE NEW

America On Line (AOL) and Time Warner merged in 1999, creating the greatest Internet and media conglomerate in the history of electronic communications. Gerald Levin, former AOL Time Warner chief executive officer (CEO), was the merger's chief architect, and he envisioned building the media company of the future. It would combine radio, television, movies, books, newspapers and magazines, and the Internet into a multimedia superpower. Once the merger was in place and his dream was realized, Levin decided to end his career. By the time he retired in 1999, however, the corporate marriage was already facing some difficult times and headed for disaster. At the time of his departure, Levin was prophetic when he said, "I have the greatest confidence in Dick Parsons' ability to lead the company forward, coalesce its diverse interests, and work with our strategic partners to achieve our ambitious goals."[1]

Richard D. Parsons became CEO of AOL Time Warner in May 2002 and chairman of the board in May 2003. Although he had helped to bring about the merger of the two companies, Parsons took charge of a new company that seemed doomed to failure. In January 2000, at the peak of dotcom bubble burst, Time Warner Inc. had agreed to be acquired by AOL in a stock swap priced at $284 billion.[2] By the time Parsons took over, the stock market valued AOL Time Warner at $61 billion. More than $223 billion in shareholder wealth had been lost.

Parson's first annual meeting as CEO of AOL Time Warner has become legendary because he faced a mass of angry shareholders with a long list of legitimate complaints. However, as Levin had predicted before he left, Parsons skillfully used tact and diplomacy to turn things around.[3] Since becoming CEO, Parsons has set the company on a solid path toward achieving sustainable growth. Under his direction, the company's stock values have increased and its debt decreased from $30 billion to $20 billion in less than one year.[4]

REVIVING A MEDIA GIANT

In September 2003, AOL Time Warner's directors voted to rename the company Time Warner, and Parsons instituted his plan to revitalize the company based on performance rather than hyperbole. He felt that the dotcom bubble burst and the poor performance of AOL warranted a name change and pursuit of a new direction. One of his first moves was to make the company sell a controlling interest in its principal music operation, Warner Music Group.[5] It sold to an investor group led by Thomas H. Lee Partners and Edgar Bronfman, Jr. This sale alone reduced Time Warner's reported net debt by approximately $2.6 billion. Parsons said he was putting the music company in capable hands because it was in the best interests of the company's shareholders and would enable the company to pursue higher growth opportunities in other lines of business. Next, he put in place the industry's most experienced and successful management team, strengthened the company's balance sheet, simplified its corporate structure, and carried out a disciplined approach to realigning the company's portfolio of assets to improve returns. In its January 2005 report on America's Best CEOs, *Institutional Investor* magazine named Parsons the top CEO in the entertainment industry.[6] Once Parsons turned the company around, he began looking for possible new merger partners and new acquisitions that would make the company profitable.

Before becoming CEO, Parsons served as the company's cochief operating officer, overseeing its content businesses (Warner Bros., New Line Cinema, Warner Music Group, and Time Warner Book Group) as well as two key corporate functions: legal and people development. Parsons joined Time Warner as its president in February 1995 and has been a member of the company's board of directors since January 1991. As president, he oversaw the company's film entertainment and music businesses and all corporate staff functions, including financial activities, legal affairs, public affairs, and administration.

FOCUSING ON PERFORMANCE INSTEAD OF RACE

Having enjoyed high achievement throughout his professional life, Parsons believes that the key to success for African Americans in the Information Age is focusing more on performance and less on race. For most of his life, Parsons felt that paying too much attention to race was silly. Since becoming one of the few Blacks to head a major multinational corporation, Parsons acknowledged that racial matters have to be addressed. Parsons has not turned his back on the African American community. He said that one of his objectives is to transform his workforce to better reflect the customers and community it serves. "We need to make more progress in our senior management ranks."[7]

Parsons believes that America is launched on the most complex, intense, and open-ended struggle to end racial discrimination.[8] In this phase, he feels that African Americans and other minorities once denied entry to the American mainstream are empowered to take their rightful places. He believes that the goal must include (1) access to quality schools, beginning in the earliest grades and leading up to entry into college; (2) access to meaningful employment and a career, especially in the information-related industries that are the growth engine of the global economy; and (3) access to capital for investment in business development, which has been perennially denied to minority entrepreneurs.

Parsons believes that in America empowerment has a color and it is the color of money.[9] So, Parsons has put his money where his mouth is when it comes to helping African Americans gain the access that he says they need. He was on the campus of one of the nations leading historically Black universities on February 16, 2005, to officially launch the Time Warner Program at Howard University's John H. Johnson School of Communications.[10] The Time

Warner Program will involve seasoned professionals from Time Warner-owned companies sharing their wisdom and skills with students. Industry professionals invited by faculty members will come on campus to interact with students in a classroom environment as part of the coursework. Students will receive up-to-the-minute insights into industry trends and standards from people whose work literally influences millions of people worldwide.

Parsons hopes to make the media and communications program at the John H. Johnson School of Communications "simply the best," which was the initial slogan of the Time Warner cable icon HBO. This program is an extension of the partnership, begun in 1999, between Time Warner and Howard University. In 1999, the Time Warner Endowed Chair was established in the Department of Radio, TV & Film at the school. Time Warner professors have included Bill Duke and Suzanne de Passe.

BIOGRAPHY

Parsons grew up in the Bedford-Stuyvesant section of Brooklyn, NY, and went on to earn the top score among all 3,600 law school graduates who took the New York State Bar exam with him in 1971.[11] Parsons graduated from the University of Hawaii, where he played varsity basketball. He earned a law degree from Albany Law School while working nights as a janitor.

Parsons served as a lawyer for New York Governor Nelson Rockefeller and followed Rockefeller to Washington, DC, when he became vice president in 1974. In 1977, Parsons returned to New York and joined Wall Street law firm Patterson, Belknap. He left the firm to become president of Dime Savings Bank. He became the bank's CEO, seeing it through a merger with Anchor Savings Bank. While leading Dime Savings Bank, Parsons assumed several corporate and civic directorships, including one on the board of Time Warner in 1991. In February 1995, Parsons joined Time Warner as the company's president. In 2001, President George W. Bush selected Parsons to cochair a commission on Social Security. In addition, Parsons worked on the transition team for Michael Bloomberg, who was elected mayor of New York City in 2001.

Parsons is chairman of the Apollo Theatre Foundation and also serves on the boards of Citigroup, Estee Lauder, Colonial Williamsburg Foundation, Museum of Modern Art, Howard University, and the Committee to Encourage Corporate Philanthropy.

NOTES

1. America On Line. (2001, December 5). *AOL Time Warner announces senior management succession plan.* Retrieved February 9, 2006, from http://media.aoltimewarner.com/media/cb_press_view.cfm?release_num=55252328.

2. Bianco, A., & Lowry, T. (2003, May 19). Can Dick Parsons rescue AOL Time Warner? *Business Week Online.* Retrieved February 9, 2006, from http://www.businessweek.com/magazine/content/03_20/b3833001_mz001.htm.

3. Yang, C. (2003, May 16). Richard Parsons leaps the first hurdle. *Business Week Online.* Retrieved February 9, 2006, from http://www.businessweek.com/bwdaily/dnflash/may2003/nf20030516_8120.htm.

4. Roberts, J. L. (2003, December 22). *Prime time for Parsons.* Retrieved February 9, 2006, from http://msnbc.msn.com/id/3706292/.

5. International Directory of Business Biographies. (n.d.). *Richard D. Parsons 1948–.* Retrieved February 9, 2006, from http://www.referenceforbusiness.com/biography/M-R/Parsons-Richard-D-1948.html.

6. Time Warner. (n.d.). *Richard D. Parsons Chairman and Chief Executive Officer, Time Warner.* Retrieved February 10, 2006, from http://www.timewarner.com/corp/management/corp_executives/bio/parsons_richard.html.

7. Dingle, D. T., & Hughes, A. (2002, February). A time for bold leadership. *Black Enterprise,* pp. 76–82.

8. Parsons, R. (2004, August 6). Speech at the Unity Conference, Washington, DC.

9. Daniels, C. (2004). *Black power inc.* Hoboken, NJ: Wiley.

10. Howard University. (2005). *Richard Parsons officially launches the Time Warner program.* Retrieved February 9, 2006, from http://www.howard.edu/schoolcommunications/NewsEvents/NewsArchive/Time-Warner.htm.

11. International Directory of Business Biographies. (n.d.). *Richard D. Parsons 1948–.* Retrieved February 9, 2006, from http://www.referenceforbusiness.com/biography/M-R/Parsons-Richard-D-1948.html.

Chapter 24

John W. Thompson
Chairman of the Board of Directors and Chief Executive Officer, Symantec Corporation

BECOMING THE BEST EXECUTIVE IN SILICON VALLEY

In spring 1999, Reverend Jesse Jackson's campaign to get more African Americans hired in Silicon Valley met with an unexpected turn of events. On April 14, 1999, the day after Jackson arrived in the high-tech capital of America, John W. Thompson was named president and CEO of Symantec Corporation, a well-known software company located in the valley. The news media seized the opportunity to report that while Jackson was berating high-tech corporate executives for not hiring more Blacks, Thompson had become the top-ranking African American executive in Silicon Valley at the same time. Although this irony made for good news stories, Thompson made it known that he did not like the publicity he was receiving as another "first Black"; he wanted it to be publicized that he was the best man for the job. Since taking over the firm, Thompson has demonstrated many times that he is not only the right man for that position but one of the best executives in the business.[1]

166

On November 14, 2005, *Fortune Magazine* included Symantec on its 2005 list of blue ribbon companies.[2] To make the list, a company had to have already been on at least four of the publication's lists during the calendar year: Fortune 1000, Global 500, 100 Best Companies to Work For, and America's Most Admired. Symantec was one of five of the blue ribbon companies that met the financial qualifications required to make both the Fortune 1000 and the 100 Fastest-Growing Companies lists. The company had large enough revenues to qualify for the Fortune 1000 list and also sustained the 25 percent revenue growth necessary to make the 100 Fastest-Growing Companies list.

Also in 2005, *CRN*, another respected trade journal, named Thompson number one on its list of the information technology (IT) industry's top 25 most influential executives.[3] Thompson had already been on the list of *Business Week*'s top managers for 2002 and listed among *Time Magazine*'s Digital 50 in 1999.[4]

Thompson has received this recognition because, under his leadership, Symantec has become one of the leading forces in the software security industry. He has turned Symantec from a $632 million consumer software company to a $1.2 billion enterprise security market leader.[5] Key government agencies and Fortune 500 companies worldwide use Symantec products. Although many Silicon Valley companies have been terminating workers, Symantec has doubled its workforce since 1999.

Thompson recognized the growing importance of information and the need to protect it. Symantec had always been a company that provided software, such as Norton antivirus products. Thompson's approach, however, has been to expand Symantec's ability to help consumers and businesses secure and manage their growing dependence on information on the Internet. With global operations in more than 40 countries, the company now provides a broad range of security, storage, availability, and performance management solutions to help customers manage their IT infrastructures.

SECURING THE NATION'S INFORMATION INFRASTRUCTURE

President George W. Bush recognized Thompson's capabilities and, in September 2002, appointed him to the National Infrastructure Advisory Committee (NIAC) to make recommendations regarding the security of America's critical information infrastructure.[6] Richard

Clarke, the president's special advisor for cyberspace security, said at the time that maintaining a secure information infrastructure was one of the nation's most urgent concerns and that Thompson's appointment provided the NIAC a proven leader with invaluable expertise in the global Internet security marketplace.

The NIAC was established by the president to provide advice on the security of information systems for information infrastructure supporting key sectors of the national economy, including banking and finance, transportation, energy, manufacturing, and emergency government services. Thompson's appointment was announced in conjunction with the establishment of the National Strategy to Secure Cyberspace.

The NIAC is charged with the task of proposing and developing ways to encourage private industry to perform periodic risk assessments of critical information and telecommunications systems. In addition, the council is directed to monitor the development of private sector Information Sharing and Analysis Centers (ISACs) and provide recommendations to the Critical Infrastructure Protection Board, chaired by Clarke, on how these organizations can best foster improved cooperation among the ISACs, the National Infrastructure Protection Center, and other federal government entities.

Thompson and his company have provided a leadership role in several homeland security initiatives, including content recommendations on the National Strategy to Secure Cyberspace. Thompson chaired the 2002 Silicon Valley Blue Ribbon Task Force on Aviation Security and Technology.[7] Under his leadership, Symantec is a founding member of the National Cyber Security Alliance, a coalition of private and public entities to raise awareness of the value of cyber security throughout the United States. Symantec is also a founding member of Information Technology Information Sharing and Analysis Center and serves on its board of directors. Thompson also served as a panel member at the president's Twenty-first Century High-Tech Forum in June 2002.

AFRICAN AMERICANS AND SUCCESS IN THE INFORMATION AGE

Thompson is currently the only African American leading a large global IT company. Although he does not want to be remembered for being the highest ranking African American in Silicon Valley, he does not avoid helping other people of color. He spoke at both of Reverend Jackson's digital connections conferences in recent years and periodically returns to Florida Agricultural and Mechanical (A&M) University, the historically Black university where he received his undergraduate business degree, to coach students. Thompson believes that African Americans must prepare themselves to perform in the Information Age and not get too focused on race.

The only limiting factor here is the commitment and conviction that one brings to the job. Can you demonstrate the kind of work commitment that we need from every one of our employees that we need to win in the marketplace? Are you excited about getting up every morning and going to work, and want to help us promote not only the products that we build, but the company that we're building? If that person has that kind of attitude that comes through in the interview, I want [that person] on my team.[8]

To do well in the IT world of today, Thompson believes that African Americans must bring something to the job that transcends gender, race, and nationality and perform in a way that others want to emulate:

But you never set out to wear your ethnicity on your sleeve. That's not the set of stars and stripes you want. What you want to wear on your sleeve is your accomplishments. So I wasn't interested in having the discussion that says, "Well, he's the first African American to lead a major Silicon Valley company." So what?[9]

Thompson said that he could not point to any overt form of discrimination that occurred in his early career. He started out as a salesman in Tampa, FL, and ended up running the largest geographic profit center for IBM, so he feels that it would be hard to say that he was discriminated against, having had that kind of career advancement: "I spent 28 years running around IBM doing a bunch of stuff, and I never even thought of myself ... Yes, I am African American, it is undeniable. But I don't think of myself in that context."[10]

BIOGRAPHY

Thompson grew up the son of a postal worker and schoolteacher in West Palm Beach, FL.[11] His parents instilled in him the concepts of hard work and preparation for life's pursuits. Thompson finished high school and went to college. He married at 19 and soon became a father. Fortunately, his professors took an interest in him, and one convinced him to work for IBM after graduation. Thompson completed his undergraduate studies at Florida A&M University and went on to get a master's degree in management science from Massachusetts Institute of Technology's Sloan School of Management.

He started working for IBM in the 1970s and sealed impressive deals as a salesman in Tampa. By 1993, he was general manager of IBM Americas, a $37 billion unit with 30,000 employees. Thompson said he still wanted to put into play all the skills he has acquired at IBM and become an industry leader. In 1999, he took over Symantec and became one of the leading IT executives in the country.

NOTES

1. Hughes, A. (2004, September). The best CEO in Silicon Valley: John Thompson has transformed Symantec into a multibillion-dollar security software juggernaut. *Black Enterprise.* Retrieved May 22, 2006, from http://www.blackenterprise.com/default.asp.

2. Brown, S. (2004, November 30). *Fortune announces 2004 list of blue-ribbon companies.* Retrieved February 8, 2006, from Fortune Press Room Web site: http://www.timeinc.net/fortune/information/Presscenter/0,,11302004_blueribbon,00.html.

3. Hooper, L. (2005, November 11). *Top 25 executives: John Thompson, Symantec.* Retrieved February 8, 2006, from CRN Web site: http://www.crn.com/sections/special/reports/top25.jhtml?ArticleID=173500420.

4. "The antivirus guardian." Retrieved February 8, 2006, from the Time Warner Web site: http://www.time.com/time/digital/digital50/43.html.

5. Saita, A. (2003, February). Profile: John Thompson. *Information Security Magazine.* Retrieved February 8, 2006, from http://infosecuritymag.techtarget.com/2003/feb/profile.shtml.

6. Symantec. (2002, September 18). *Bush appoints Symantec chairman/CEO to security panel.* Retrieved February 8, 2006, from http://www.symantec.com/press/2002/n020918a.html.

7. City of San Jose. (2002, February 27). *Airport Security Technology Task Force taps Symantec CEO John W. Thompson as working chair.* Retrieved February 8, 2006, from http://www.sanjoseca.gov/cityManager/releases/airportceo.html.

8. The Black Collegian Online. (n.d.). *Tips for entering the IT industry.* Retrieved February 8, 2006, from http://www.black-collegian.com/career/career-reports/tip2000-1st.shtml.

9. Symantec Corp. (2004, January 4). *On the record: John Thompson.* Retrieved February 9, 2006, from the SFGate Web site: http://www. sfgate.com/cgi-bin/article.cgi?f=/c/a/2004/01/04/BUG78426I51.DTL.

10. Kirby, C. (2002, January 29). *John Thompson: Man with a plan: Symantec prospering in Thompson era.* Retrieved February 8, 2006, from the SFGate Web site: http://www.sfgate.com/cgi-bin/article.cgi?file=/chronicle/archive/2002/01/29/BU53763.DTL.

11. Saita, A. (2003, February). Profile: John Thompson. *Information Security Magazine.* Retrieved February 8, 2006, from http://infosecuritymag. techtarget.com/2003/feb/profile.shtml.

Chapter 25

Robert L. Johnson

Founder and Former Chief Executive Officer, Black Entertainment Television

PUTTING CORPORATE POWER INTO THE BLACK INTERNET

Over a 25-year period, Robert L. Johnson built the largest Black-owned media company that America had ever seen. Johnson spun off his earnings from Black Entertainment Television (BET) into numerous other ventures, including restaurants, nightclubs, and even airlines. When he decided to use the technology of the Information Revolution to expand his media empire even further, he did so in two ways. First, he used corporate power and influence to launch a portal for African Americans that would make BET the number one Black location on the Web. Next, he moved much of his BET programming to the digital cable television tier and increased his audience and his profits. These moves, coupled with all of his other ventures, made Johnson America's first Black billionaire and one of the nation's leading media moguls in the Information Age.[1]

To build his Web site, Johnson attracted the largest investment in a Black-owned Internet company ever. One of the key investors, Microsoft's chief executive officer (CEO) Bill Gates, said at that time: "I believe Black Entertainment Television and Microsoft will help to make the Internet and the interactive entertainment industry a place that is exciting for all consumers."[2]

Johnson obtained more than $30 million in start-up funding from Microsoft, USA Networks, News Corp., and AT&T's Liberty Digital. Earlier in 1997, BET had already launched its first effort in cyberspace with MSBET.com. That Web site was the result of a joint venture between BET and Microsoft. MSBET was little more than a showcase for programming that was on the cable network. Launched in 1999 and dubbed BET.com, the new Web site featured comprehensive news for the African American community, chat technology, and a retail area catering to Black consumers. The site generated revenue through advertising and e-commerce.[3] The site was designed to increase the number of African Americans using the Internet. Since its launch, it has drawn more than 1 million viewers and proven that African Americans will use sites that are geared to their interests.[4–7]

CAPITALIZING ON DIGITAL CABLE

Turning the Internet into a successful and lucrative enterprise was not Johnson's first venture into the digital arena. As the founder and CEO of BET, he took a business that he started in his basement and tuned into a media conglomerate while branching out into ancillary businesses. In the digital world, he was also one of the first in the Black community to capitalize on digital cable networking to expand his BET programming.

"Digital opens more doors for programming choices for customers, and we have a strong brand that we can leverage to bring those choices to our target audience," Johnson said.[8] He pointed out that BET on Jazz and BET Gospel are excellent examples of that notion. He predicted that when the digital offerings on cable TV get greater penetration, brands like BET that have strong market position, good management, and the ability to leverage the analog business for promotion will be in an advantageous position. He concluded that the cable industry "needs to recognize that diversity in the digital world is as important as diversity in the analog world." BET Digital

Networks was created in 1996 and now consists of a suite that includes BET on Jazz, which has 7 million subscribers; BET International, reaching 4 million homes; as well as the new offering BET Gospel, which features the participation of local churches.

THE INTERNET IS JUST ANOTHER WAY FOR
BLACK PEOPLE TO COMMUNICATE

Johnson does not take the usual view on African Americans and the Information Revolution. He believes that African American audiences will always respond to things that service their needs and that they adopt technology very quickly:

You look at cable penetration in African American households. Look at the VCR, telephone: African Americans probably spend more for long distance telephone per capita than any other population. Beepers, cell phones, the technology has to serve their needs. The African American people love to communicate, and they do it orally. They don't do a whole lot of letter writing, but they will definitely go to the long distance phone and check in with their extended families, distant relatives, and friends. The same thing with the beeper or the cell phone.[9]

Johnson feels that the Black community must avail itself of Internet resources to succeed in the Information Age. He pledged to use the resources of BET to create an online destination that will educate, enrich, empower, and entertain African Americans. Johnson feels that in the future African Americans must be shown how the Internet can service them the way other technologies do. What he tried to do with BET.com was let African Americans know that the Internet is just another way for them to communicate and obtain information. He does not believe that money is a deterrent. In an interview with Jeremy M. Brosowsky, Johnson outlined his view of African Americans and new age communication technology.

I'm not worried about the cost factor. African Americans spend on average 30 bucks a month on cable, 50 bucks a month for long distance service. I'm not worried about the economics. What you have to do is demystify the computer, and then let them know that there's content on the Internet that's specifically geared and tailored to their interests, and you've got to promote it.

Johnson cites economic racism as one of the deterrents for African Americans not being on the Internet.

When you look at a market, and you know there's money to be made in a market, but you ignore it because you don't want to be associated with or involved in the market, that's what I call economic racism. It's a little bit of being ignorant and stupid about the marketplace, and a lot of it's about being arrogant about the marketplace. So you stay away from it. Many Black businesses started because White businesses wouldn't get in that business. North Carolina Mutual, the granddaddy of Black businesses, was in the insurance business because nobody would write policies for Black people. So what I'm saying is the Internet people have yet to wake up to the fact that African Americans spend $500 billion on consumer goods, and a lot of those dollars go into entertainment and communications. The long distance people got it.

Johnson believes that Internet moguls feel that that Black people are not worth the effort.

That's the economic racism. They simply think "Black people can't afford computers, Black people don't understand computers, they don't know how to work them, and therefore we're wasting our money going after them." I encountered the same thing when I started BET. I'd go in to sell Madison Avenue on advertising on BET on cable. They'd say, "First of all, the big cities aren't wired," which was partly true. That's the access issue. "And two, Black people can't afford cable; cable costs 30 bucks a month." That's the can't-afford-it. But what the cable operators found out was just the opposite.

Johnson created BET.com to let African Americans know that there is a gateway to the Internet and that it can be used to communicate but also to stimulate additional businesses in the Black community.

BIOGRAPHY

Johnson was born April 8, 1946, in Hickory, MS, but spent almost all of his childhood in Freeport, IL. He was the ninth of ten children born to Archie and Edna Johnson. Johnson studied history at the University of Illinois and graduated in 1968 with a bachelor's degree. He earned a master's degree in public administration at Princeton University in 1972.

Johnson worked at the Corporation for Public Broadcasting and the Washington Urban League before becoming press secretary for Walter E. Fauntroy, who was the congressional delegate from the District of Columbia.[10]

Johnson moved from that position in 1976 to serve as vice president of government relations for the National Cable & Telecommunications

Association (NCTA), a trade association representing more than 1,500 cable television companies. In 1979, he left NCTA to create BET, the first cable television network aimed at African Americans, which launched in January 1980, broadcasting for 2 hours a week. Eleven years later, BET became the first Black-controlled company listed on the New York Stock Exchange.

In April 1997, BET teamed up with Chevy Chase Bank to offer a BET Visa credit card to African Americans nationwide. In this partnership, the bank could pursue its goal of doing business with more African Americans and BET could begin to build BET Financial Services, a new company that planned to offer mortgage and brokerage services, mutual funds, and home equity loans. To run the company, Johnson teamed with Alma Brown, the widow of the late secretary of commerce Ronald H. Brown, one of the highest ranking Blacks of the presidential administration of Bill Clinton.

During the same period, BET also opened a chain of restaurants called BET Soundstage. With Bell Atlantic, BET planned to test market packages of telecommunications services designed to meet the needs of African American consumers. The alliance was designed to help Bell Atlantic reach the African American community and extend BET's brand name into the telecommunications marketplace.

During the 1990s, Johnson unsuccessfully attempted to build a sports arena in downtown Washington, DC, and to buy a discount airline. However, his success in early 2003 shocked many around the world. The National Basketball Association's Board of Governors officially chose him as the first Black majority owner of a franchise team in Charlotte, NC: the Charlotte Bobcats, which began play in fall 2004. It is poetic justice that a Black man owns a basketball team, because the sport is one that African Americans reinvented and continue to dominate.

In 1998, Johnson took BET private, buying back all of its publicly traded stock. A year later, Viacom bought BET for $2.3 billion in stock. Johnson continued to be the company's chairman and CEO. He also serves on the boards of US Airways, General Mills, and Hilton Hotels. In 2000, when Johnson sold BET to Viacom, he became the first Black billionaire. However, Johnson never rested on his laurels.

In an attempt to create the country's largest black-owned asset management firm, in 2005 Johnson launched RLJ Equity Partners and RLJ Select Investments.[11] RLJ Equity Partners is a private equity joint venture with the Carlyle Group. RLJ Select Investments is a hedge fund joint venture with Deutsche Asset Management. Shortly after setting up these firms, Johnson retired from BET.

NOTES

1. Pulley, B. (2004). *The billion dollar BET*. Hoboken, NJ: Wiley.

2. Microsoft. (1996, February 1). *Black Entertainment Television and Microsoft announce new alliance*. Retrieved February 10, 2006, from http://www.microsoft.com/presspass/press/1996/feb96/msbetpr.mspx.

3. Rawlinson, R. (1999, October 6). *Can Robert Johnson bring more Blacks online?* Retrieved February 10, 2006, from Salon.com Web site: http://www.salon.com/tech/feature/1999/10/06/bet_johnson/index.html.

4. Seminerio, M. (1999, August 12). *Attacking the "digital divide"? You BET*. Retrieved February 10, 2006, from the ZDNet Web site: http://news.zdnet.com/2100-9595_22-515417.html?legacy=zdnn.

5. DC Internet Staff. (2001, January 9). *BET.com hits 1 million unique viewers*. Retrieved February 10, 2006, from http://dc.internet.com/news/print.php/554401.

6. "BET ranked No. 1 Web site for African-Americans." (2001, January 11). *Washington Business Journal*. Retrieved February 10, 2006, from http://www.bizjournals.com/washington/stories/2001/01/08/daily21.html.

7. Swibel, M. (1999, December 10). BET.com prepares for $6M ad blitz. *Washington Business Journal*. Retrieved February 10, 2006, from http://www.bizjournals.com/washington/stories/1999/12/13/story5.html.

8. CableWorld Staff. (2000, May 15). *Going strong at 20*. Retrieved February 10, 2006, from http://www.cableworld.com/cgi/cw/show_mag.cgi?pub=cw&mon=051500&file=going_strong.inc.

9. Lohr, G. A. (2001, April 27). BET unit lays off workers, streamlines programming. *Washington Business Journal*. Retrieved February 10, 2006, from http://www.bizjournals.com/washington/stories/2001/04/30/story7.html.

10. Barber, J. T., & Tait, A. A. (2001). The new model of Black entrepreneurship: BET Holdings, Inc. In J. T. Barber & A. A. Tait (Eds.), *The information society and the Black community* (pp. 111–126). Westport, CT: Praeger.

11. Killian, E. (2006, February 1). BET founder hires industry vets to lead investment team. *Washington Business Journal*. Retrieved February 10, 2006, from http://www.bizjournals.com/washington/stories/2006/01/30/daily27.html.

Chapter 26

Noah A. Samara

Chairman and Chief Executive Officer, WorldSpace Satellite Radio

BRINGING THE DIGITAL REVOLUTION TO THE THIRD WORLD

One morning, more than a decade ago, a telecommunications lawyer named Noah Samara read in the morning newspaper that AIDS was spreading rapidly through Africa because the continent lacked infrastructure to alert people about the epidemic. The article predicted a catastrophe of holocaust proportions. Samara realized that Africans were dying not just of disease. They were dying from lack of information. This incident changed Samara's life, and since then he has worked to build a communications network that will provide Africa and other third world regions with the information needed for people to enjoy a better quality of life.

In 1990, Samara founded WorldSpace to provide digital satellite audio, data, and multimedia services primarily to the emerging markets of Africa and Asia. The company's mission was to provide a variety of high-quality programming through a subscription-based digital radio service that uses low-cost portable satellite radios to service markets that lack programming choices. WorldSpace is the first and only company with rights to the world's globally allocated spectrum for digital satellite radio. Its broadcast footprint covers more than 130 countries, including all of Africa, India, China, the Middle East, and most of Western Europe, an area that includes 5 billion people and more than 300 million automobiles.

BUILDING THE INFRASTRUCTURE

A pioneer of digital satellite radio, Samara has made WorldSpace the company that first brought the concept of satellite radio to the world. The WorldSpace satellite network is now composed of operational satellites that service three large geographic areas. Each satellite has three beams, and each beam is able to send up to 80 channels directly to portable satellite radios. Inside each World-Space digital satellite radio is a proprietary chipset designed to lock onto the WorldSpace network.

In 1995, Samara obtained $10 million from Middle Eastern investors, which enabled WorldSpace to begin negotiating with vendors and potential customers. Soon the company announced agreements with Hitachi, JVC, Matsushita Electric Industrial, and Sanyo Technosound to make the custom radios for WorldSpace. France's Alcatel Alsthom and SGS-Thomson developed satellites and microprocessors for the fledgling system.[1–3]

WorldSpace now sells subscriptions to its radio service and receivers and leases broadcast capacity on AfriStar and AsiaStar, the satellites that it owns.[4] It does not compete with XM Satellite Radio Holdings Inc. or Sirius Satellite Radio Inc., which hold the only two U.S. satellite radio broadcast licenses. Samara was instrumental, however, in the development of the satellite radio industry through his early involvement with XM Satellite Radio in the United States. WorldSpace created the initial proprietary technology and programming infrastructure that are used by both WorldSpace Satellite Radio and XM Satellite Radio. WorldSpace was one of XM's original investors in the mid-1990s and licensed technology to XM. It sold its stake in XM in 1999 for $75 million. WorldSpace aims to apply the business model pioneered by XM and Sirius in the United States to Africa and other parts of the world. By 2004, WorldSpace reported revenue of $8.5 million, down from $13 million for 2003, according to SEC filings. It posted net losses of $577 million in 2004 and $217 million in 2003. In 2005, WorldSpace registered an initial public offering of $100 million of stock with the Securities and Exchange Commission (SEC).

Capturing investments to fund Samara's ambitious projects has met with difficulty and controversy. Saudi investors Mohammed H. Al Amoudi, one of the world's richest men, and Khalid Bin Mahfouz, a former chief operating officer of the Bank of Credit and Commerce International, have provided about $1 billion to WorldSpace, according to *The Washington Post*.[5] Both men have been accused of financially supporting the al Qaeda terrorist network, a charge they have denied. A third investor, Salah Idris, was the owner of a factory in Sudan that the United States bombed in 1998.

In December 2004, the company raised $155 million in private investment and restructured its debt, allowing WorldSpace to begin a subscription radio service in India. It now has 53,000 subscribers, including 22,000 in India, who pay between $3 and $5 monthly to receive up to 80 channels of news, music, and sports programs. XM and Sirius, by contrast, combined have about 5 million subscribers.

As a result of the debt restructuring, Al Amoudi, the Bin Mahfouz family, and Idris no longer hold any direct debt or equity interest in WorldSpace or have any voting control. However, if WorldSpace makes a profit between now and 2015, the company has to pay a royalty to Stonehouse Capital Ltd., a company controlled by two sons of Bin Mahfouz, according to the company's SEC filing. Under a recent agreement, Idris holds only nonvoting shares in Yenura, a company that owns shares in WorldSpace. Yenura is controlled by WorldSpace founder and chief executive Noah Samara, who is the company's major shareholder.

In 2005, XM Satellite Radio Holdings Inc. invested $25 million in WorldSpace to broaden XM's reach and help turn satellite radio into a global service similar to satellite television.[6] The two companies agreed to work together to develop products such as receivers and to strengthen relationships with distributors such as automakers and sources of programming. On the heels of the XM announcement, WorldSpace's underwriter raised the projected IPO share price from $16 to $18 per share to $18 to $20 according to *The Washington Post*.

SERVING THE INFORMATION HAVE-NOTS

Despite all the big money deals, Samara remains a media mogul with a purpose. Speaking before the International Telecommunications

Union (ITU), the United Nations Economic Commission Africa, and other world organizations, Samara has talked about his method for using technology to assist Africa and other socially and economically depressed parts of the world.[7,8] At the ITU's special session on the digital divide, he said there are practical, easy-to-close global information gaps.

Over the last 10 years, we at WorldSpace developed a simple solution to help bridge the digital divide. We launched two satellites over Africa, the Middle East, and Asia to broadcast digital audio and multimedia content directly from the satellites to an inexpensive receiver. How is this system actually bridging the digital divide? We have a broadcast today called the Africa Learning Channel that is reaching an actual audience of 6 million people with education and information on critical subjects such as HIV/AIDS along with structured programs for women on microenterprise. We are deploying WorldSpace receivers in every school in Kenya with the Kenya Institute of Education to continuously train teachers and supplement the daily education of the students. The deployment will be complete in May of this year, allowing us to reach 11 million Kenyan students every day. And after school hours, we plan to use the receivers to deliver audio-drama, infotainment, and education to adults and professionals.[9]

He concluded that in all WorldSpace projects the company is focused on creating information affluence and measurably bridging the digital divide. To this end, WorldSpace receivers are more than just digital radios. Because they contain microprocessors, they can perform many of the functions of a computer. WorldSpace offers many services that one cannot get over traditional radios.[10] Some of these services include Web casting auxiliary educational content to supplement regular instructional material while simultaneously ensuring that unwanted and inappropriate content on the Internet is kept beyond reach of the students. It also offers multicasting through a data port that transforms the radio into a wireless modem able to download data to personal computers at rates of up to 128 kbps. In addition, Net2Radio is an e-mail application that allows an Internet-based user to send a 255-character e-mail message via the Internet to a single WorldSpace recipient or group of WorldSpace recipients within the AsiaStar and AfriStar coverage area who are not on the Internet. The recipient receives the text message via a WorldSpace receiver interfaced to a personal computer (PC). The end user automatically prompts to view the e-mail once received through the PC's notepad application.

The network also offers Combined Live Audio and Slide Show, an innovative solution developed specifically to address distance education requirements in developing countries. It uses live satellite broadcasting to deliver synchronous and asynchronous e-learning content beyond the reach of Internet, telephone lines, and mail delivery. It supports live lectures based on PowerPoint presentations with the possibility of real-time annotations.

Finally, WorldSpace offers a global information and emergency broadcast system for 155 countries, equipping organizations with the ability to broadcast urgent, time-sensitive messages warning of threats to user groups.

BIOGRAPHY

Noah A. Samara was born in Ethiopia in 1956 and was raised there as well as in Tanzania. His Sudanese father was a teacher and a diplomat.[11] He moved from his country when he was 17 to pursue education, leaving only weeks before a revolution, a period of terror, in Ethiopia killed many of his close friends. "But for the grace of God," he said, "I could have gone the way of my friends."[12]

He was educated in England and the United States and eventually earned a Doctor of Jurisprudence from Georgetown University Law School. Samara began to develop the vision that information was the key to expanding opportunities.

Samara's early career was in satellite telecommunications, first with Geostar Corporation and later with the Washington law firm of Venable, Baetjer, Howard & Civiletti. He has been involved in development of both geostationary and low-earth-orbit satellite systems since the mid-1980s. He was an advisor to numerous global telecommunications and broadcasting organizations on a wide range of business and regulatory issues.

Business Week, Newsweek, The London Times, Billboard, and *The Washington Post,* among other major publications, have profiled Samara. *Africa International* magazine awarded Samara its 1997 Innovation Trophy for his development of the WorldSpace system. In 2000, Samara received the Peace Through Education award from the Pacem In Terris Institute of La Roche College.

Samara is a recognized leader in bringing satellite to America and the rest of the world. He has published articles in the fields of satellite communications and international law. Noah Samara has served as the chairman, chief executive officer, and president of

WorldSpace and its predecessors since inception. Samara is married and has two children. He is an avid reader, enjoying a range of work from technical journals to classical literature, and also plays golf.

NOTES

1. Yang, C., & Johnston, M. (1997, June 23). Media mogul for the third world. *Businessweek*. Retrieved February 11, 2006, from http://www. businessweek.com/1997/26/b353373.htm.

2. WorldSpace. (1998, December 9). *WorldSpace Corporation & manufacturing partners Hitachi, JVC, Matsushita (Panasonic), and Sanyo unveil world's first digital satellite radio receivers*. Retrieved February 12, 2006, from http://64.233.179.104/search?q=cache:6TfCOSco0YQJ:www.worldspace. com/press/releases/1999/12_09_98.html+WorldSpace+Hitachi+JVC+% 22press+room%22&hl=en&gl=us&ct=clnk&cd=1.

3. Swibel, M. (1999, October 15). In race to satellite radio, WorldSpace finishes first. *Washington Business Journal*. Retrieved February 12, 2006, from http://washington.bizjournals.com/washington/stories/1999/10/18/ newscolumn5.html.

4. WorldSpace. (1999, October 21). *WorldSpace launches the world's largest digital audio broadcast system, providing unprecedented coverage across African continent*. Retrieved February 12, 2006, from http:// 64.233.179.104/search?q=cache:YAtJ13nk0jsJ:www.worldspace.com/press/ releases/1999/10_21_99.html+WorldSpace+launches+the+World%27s+ largest+%22press+room%22&hl=en&gl=us&ct=clnk&cd=1.

5. Shin, A. (2005, April 19). WorldSpace sets stock offering. *The Washington Post*. Retrieved February 12, 2006, from http://www.washingtonpost. com/wp-dyn/articles/A63988-2005Apr18.html.

6. Shin, A. (2005, July 20). XM invests $25 million in rival WorldSpace. *The Washington Post*. Retrieved February 12, 2006, from http://www. washingtonpost.com/wp-dyn/content/article/2005/07/19/AR20050719017 68_pf.html.

7. Samara, N. (2000, October 14). Remarks from a speech presented at the African Enterprise Networks Millennium Conference, Addis Ababa, Ethiopia.

8. Samara, N. (2001, June 18). *Ethiopia in the knowledge age*. Speech presented to the United Nations Economic Commission for Africa, Addis Ababa, Ethiopia.

9. Samara, N. (2002, March 18). *Practical approaches to bridging the digital divide*. Speech presented at the Digital Divide Special Session of the International Telecommunication Union, Istanbul, Turkey.

10. WorldSpace. (n.d.). *About WorldSpace*. Retrieved February 12, 2006, from http://www.worldspace.com/about/.

11. Center for Strategic and International Studies. (n.d.). *Advisory board member. Seven revolutions.* Retrieved February 12, 2006, from http://7revs.csis.org/AdvisoryCommittee/b_samara.htm.

12. Samara, N. (1999, October 25). Speech presented at the African Development Forum, Addis Ababa, Ethiopia.

Index

access: to capital for investment, 163; to communications technologies, 64–65; to computers, 41, 47, 86, 95–96; to meaningful employment, 163; to quality schools, 163; to technology, 13
achievement, model of, 154–55
Adelphi University, 55, 143
Africa Learning Channel, 181
Africana.com, 152–53
Africana Encyclopedia, 152
African Americans: adopting technology quickly, 174; attractiveness of, to employers, 27; bringing accomplishments to the job, 169; cyberspace advancing, 127–28; cyberspace for, 135–36; economic racism as a deterrent for, 174–75; empowering communities with networks, 113; future of computing and, 14; global communications policies and, 36; high-tech companies owned by, 78; high-tech jobs and, 60, 75; hiring of, 6; impact of future on, 120; as industry leaders, 159; Information Age and, 71–72; Internet service for, 140; Internet use and, 26; involvement of, in IT industry, 21; Kennard's views on digital age and, 65; level playing field for, 20; leveraging consumer power, 78; mastering Internet, 133; mastery of

computing and, 13–14; as overrepresented in unskilled jobs, 26–27; Powell's views on, 71–72; preparation of, for Information Age, 102–3; success of, in Information Age, 168–69. *See also* Black community; digital divide
African American Studies, 125
Africana Studies Program, University of Toledo, 125
African Encarta Reference Suite, 152
AfriStar, 179
Al Amoudi, Mohammed H., 180
Albany Law School, 164
Albert R. Wynn and Associates, 61
The Algebra Project, 112, 115
Alkalimat, Dr. Abdul, 107, 124–30
Alto personal computer, 11–12
America On Line (AOL), 133, 134, 141, 152, 153, 161
Andreessen, Marc, 140
AntiRacismNet, 137, 138
AOL Key Audiences, Turner as general manager of, 153
AOL Time Warner, 159, 162–63
Appiah, Kwame Anthony, 152
Apple Corporation, 12
Applied Physics Laboratory, 89
architecture of desktop computers, 17–18
architecture of information, 12
Army, U.S., 72–73

About the Author

JOHN T. BARBER is the Deputy Chief Learning Officer of the Ballistic Missile Defense University in Washington, D.C., and an Adjunct Professor in the Communications Department at George Mason University in Fairfax, Virginia. Dr. Barber has more than twenty-five years of experience as a media analyst, communications educator and scholar, and broadcasting practitioner. His previous book, *The Information Society and the Black Community* (Praeger, 2000), was one of the first to provide a comprehensive examination of the prospects and pitfalls of a historically disadvantaged group in a period of rapid technological advances and economic growth in America.